Growin' Up in Little Dixie

by

H. Tom Gardner

ISBN: 0-75962-627-8

This book is printed on acid free paper.

1stBooks - rev. 06/27/01

Introduction

I received a lot of wonderful help from all the members of my family in recalling the details of events so I could accurately reconstruct stories that occurred years ago. This is a true story of the basic culture that existed in Little Dixie during the great depression, one of the most trying times in our nations history. It certainly reflects the events in our family's history, mostly very good I would say, maybe a little bad here and there. Everyone had to struggle mightily to keep his spirits and his head above the flood waters of hopelessness. The depression showed no favors; everyone was being sucked down into the vortex of poverty and dispair.

There were millions of good people that didn't have the means that the poorest of the poor have today. They had no hope of having any goodness to look forward to. Nearly every day a freight train would come through our town. Many times it would have a hundred bums hanging all over it. They were headed "just somewhere", looking for something that would improve their lives. Most all of them were looking for a job, any job. Most had nothing or maybe some would have a few pieces of bread and a quart of jelly. Maybe they had a little can of peaches some one gave them. They didn't worry if they had a balanced diet or not, just so long as it filled their bellies. These guy were not bums, not in the way the name suggest, they were good family men trying to find a way, just any way to feed their families and to better their place in life.

This is not the story of some ancient civilization that existed in the far past, trying to cope with the problems they had in providing for their needs. This is the story of those of us living now who are a little older than we want to admit. But our history was real and we had to cope with it the best we could. I hope it is not repeated because the future generations think it cannot happen to them. It can and it will, if we let greed and lust play fast and loose with the principals of honesty, decency, and good character, and especially if we don't keep a somewhat soft spot in our hearts for the other fellow.

Where is the territory that is called "Little Dixie"? Well, it is generally the same territory that the Indian nations occupied before Oklahoma statehood. They were located along the Texas and Arkansas borders in the southeastern corner of Oklahoma. The Choctaws, Cherokees, Chickasaws, Creeks and Seminoles, along with a scattering of other Indian tribes were moved into the Oklahoma territory in the middle to latter part of the 1800's.

They started rebuilding their lives and businesses. They established new governments and councils, they formed what was known as "Indian nations". Most of the members of the smaller tribes, from the southern parts of the USA, were relocated in various other parts of Oklahoma . The orginal governments, that had been formed by the 5 civilized tribes when they first arrived in the Indian territory, were dissolved. In 1907 the Indian nations were absorbed into the United States, along with other sections of the territory, to form the new state of Oklahoma.

Members of the 5 civilized tribes were gradually becoming educated and financially self sufficient, considering their frontier circumstances, and in some cases they were very well to do. Some of them owned businesses, big farms and other fundamental elements of industry in the state they were moved to. They had taken up the white mans business methods and were on their way to being successful citizens.

They were forced to leave their holdings in Georgia, Alabama and Florida when the federal government confiscated their property and expelled them to the unsettled territory of Oklahoma. To get here, they traveled along the "Trail of Tears", as they called it, because thousands of them died from the hardships and difficulties they endured along the way. For the most part, they walked the entire distance. They had to carry all their possessions on their backs or in wagons, if they had one, or on horseback and whatever devices they could find.

I was very fortunate to be one of the "white eyes" [a general slang word they had for the whites]. I had personal contacts with some of the descendants and others who I believe were some of the original victims of the "Trail of Tears" ordeal. The state of Oklahoma was established in 1907 and was only 15 years old when I was born. As I grew up, it wasn't unusual for our family to know Indian grownups who walked, or had been carried, over the trail as infants in their mothers arms; or rather on their backs as Indian mothers usually did.

One old Indian gentleman I knew was Mr. Edmond Gardner who lived in Valliant. He may have actually come to Oklahoma as a young boy or young adult on the trail. He was an old man in the early 1930s. He was an important and respected man in his tribe. He had created an alphabet for his tribal language. He had been on several councils when this country was an Indian nation. He had made a working radio by himself before 1934. When I saw it, it filled 3 or 4 drawers in a large cabinet. He was also a jeweler and a professional clock maker.

All these skills were years ahead of the rest of us. In the late 20's and early 30's we were listening to a tiny crystal radio by putting it in a large crock mixing bowl to amplify the sound. Then we put our ear up real close to the edge of the bowl. That way 3 or 4 guys could listen to the radio at the same time. It was kept down in the barber shop down town. That's where the guy type action was in my town.

When my mother, Rennie Mae Reynolds was growing up in Valliant, Oklahoma , they were quite often "raided" by the Indians from up in the Quachita mountains. She said nearly every saturday night they would ride their horses through town at full speed , shouting and hollering and generally boozing it up and raising hell. They weren't out to really harm anyone, but I figure they were pushing it as far as they could without getting into real trouble with the law. Mother said she and her family, for sure, stayed inside of the house when granddad was gone. They would hid under their bed when the Indians were acting up. I imagine the Indians were still ticked off having the "white eyes" to contend with.

* * * * * *

The new state of Oklahoma had not had time to fully develop its personality as a part of the nation. When I was still in grade school, the thought was that most of the people that lived in Little Dixie country had escaped from prison or were bootleggers and running from the law; or were just "poor white trash" that had moved in from elsewhere.

To some extent I suppose that thought was true. Southeast Oklahoma was a poor country even before the depression hit. There was no industrial base to provide employment for the citizens. Most everyone was or had been a poor sand—hill sharecropper or a rosin—belly pine tree logger. There were a few "rich" land owners there. Those, who had enough money when they came bought large portions of the Red River bottom land for $10 or $12 an acre. Some of it less than $5.00 an acre. They did ok in spite of the depression that came later. Red River bottom land was really good land for cotton farming.

Later in life, we came to know a family who was very wealthy. The old gentleman had made a lot of money in this poor country. His wife was wealthy in her own right. But she had died a number of years earlier. The folk lore around the neighborhood was that she had died of malnutrition. She would not spend enough money for food to keep her alive. Of course no one knew for a fact what her problem really was. However, he was a very pleasant and friendly man. I did spend a lot of time with him when I was a young man.

One day I asked him how he had managed to make so much money in this poor country, especially during the depression years when every one was so destitute. "well, Tom, I'll tell you. I wasn't such a money maker, but I was one hell of a money saver! When I came to this country I brought a little money with me. So I could take advantage of the good investments I found here, especially buying land. I started buying up large pieces of Red River bottom land as it came on the market. Much of it I got for less than $5.00 an acre. I paid $.50 and acre for some of it. In a few cases, during the depression I bought some of the marginal land for $.10 an acre. I started raising cotton. Also, I had a large number of acres in corn. I was a good farmer and I saved every penny I could possibly save. I built a cotton gin here in Idabel and started ginning cotton for all the farmers. I made some money in the farming business".

However, he also made money during the depression. For a while there, the state and county governments had no cash to pay their employees who worked on the roads, the teaches in the schools, nor the employees that worked in our state offices. The state paid their salaries with "vouchers" or "chits". They were really worthless at the time because the state and county had no money in the banks. He also got into the business of buying those vouchers and chits from the state employees, mainly the teachers, for as little as $.15 on the dollar. He had to keep them for several years, but as the conditions got better and WW11 pushed the economy up, he told me he took all those vouchers and chits to Oklahoma City and they gave him 100%

of their face value in cash. He said, "I did very well with that investment. At the time, I had little hope that they would be worth something, sometime in the future."

* * * * * *

My grandfather, on my mothers side, Thomas C.

Reynolds, did very well during the great depression. He was not rich but he was considered as "well to do" and was one of the "pillars" of the little town of Valliant, Oklahoma , where he lived. He moved his family into the Indian territory about a year before statehood. He started out as a watch maker and merchant in the little town of Sawyer, Oklahoma . He was one of the 'escapees' that came to the territory because he was somewhat dissatisfied with the hunting laws of Buford, Georgia, where he came from.

My father, Henry Cash Gardner, was a young army veteran. He was raised across the Red River, in Woodland, Texas, a little town just outside of Clarksville, Texas. He had been discharged from the army after WW1. He was working for the Frisco railroad that ran along the southern edge of Oklahoma . We have very little knowledge of where his parents came from before Texas.

He was stationed at the Valliant, Oklahoma railway station. That's where he met my mother. His parents, John Pascal Gardner and Ida Lee Graves Gardner, were also "pretty well off" during the 1890's. My grandfather, John P. Gardner was a cattle man. He lived around Clarksville, or Woodland Texas. When my father was about 4 or 5 years old his father John Paskell was killed , or rather murdered in cold blood.

As the family folklore has it, the guy that killed him was a crooked cattle buyer who resold the cattle to the Indian agency, somewhere near Clarksville, Texas. One day the buyer came out to his ranch near Woodland, Texas to buy cattle for the agency. My grandfather, John Gardner, refused to sell to him. He had discovered that the buyer had been cheating the Indian agency, supposedly, by getting a kickback. The buyer kept insisting; my grandfather still refused to sell him any more cows. After he had refused to yield to the buyers demands, he turned to ride off. The Indian cow buyer was so angered with the refusal, he pulled his gun and shot him in the back. My grandfather died immediately. That occurred some time in the late 1800's. As near as we know in 1893.

He left my grandmother with 3 small children.

Another version of the incident, and not necessarily contradictory, was told to my mother, by an elderly transit boarder in our hotel in Boswell, Oklahoma . One day in the middle 1920's he had registered at our hotel, when he found out my father's name was Gardner and that he was from near Clarksville, Texas, the stranger related his version of grandfathers murder to my mother. He said that he was part of drunken Indian raiding party that killed Mr. Gardner and took his horses and a bunch of his cattle from his corral. He said they were drunk and did the whole thing on an impulse. He assured mother that he didn't kill Mr. Gardner but that a member of the raiding party by the name of Bohannan did kill him.

After my grandfather's death, my grandmother, whose maiden name was Ida Lee Graves, returned temporarily to the little town of Vanndale, Arkansas . Granddad and she had property and family members that were still living there. After clearing up thier estate, she returned to Texas where she eventually married a Mr. Charley England, a local merchant.

He and she finished raising her family in a little village near Paris Texas.

I was born in 1922, in Boswell Oklahoma . I suppose my parents were transferred to the Boswell Oklahoma rail station almost immediately after they were married. Boswell had changed very little from the conditions that existed there before statehood. We were still surrounded by the characters that had moved to Oklahoma to escape whatever was about to happen to them.

Southeastern Oklahoma is, to this day, a unique, quiet, wilderness type of country. The politicians and some older locals still call it "Little Dixie". The railroad that went through our county was the "Frisco". Some time they called it the "Katy Line". It is still there. My father worked for them for 20 or so years. We moved up and down the line from Boswell to Rogers, Arkansas during that time. Quite often he would get "bumped" off his job by some one with more seniority than he. That was how we happened to move so much. The depression made it very hard to keep a steady job. He was finally laid off permanently, and consequently lost all of his seniority and retirement Benefits, just before he could have retired. I have no respect for the railroad company for doing that.

The railroad company has changed very little since that time. For a few years during the depression, little or no traffic was carried on the Frisco. They then ran the "Dinky" for a while . It was a combination mail, freight and passenger train. It had only one freight car. The engine was built right in. After a few years of that, a .little short freight train started running. At Swink, Oklahoma , one of the little towns along the Frisco. They would stop their train at this greasy spoon cafe on the nearby highway. The crew would get out of the engine, go over to the cafe, eat their lunch, walk back to the train, get in, and toot their whistle and off they would go.

There is very little farming in Little Dixie anymore. The sand—hill farms have been converted to cattle ranches. Most of the original farmer's children have turned into cattlemen or contractors of some sort. They have bought cowboy boots and a pickup and are now making a living by going to the nearest cafe and having breakfast or coffee every morning. That way the little woman can get the kids off to school and get to her job on time, without him getting in her way.

I do remember that all of us, who lived in "Little Dixie", blamed President Hoover and the Republicans for all our financial problems. I know some older people who still blame him. There are some really hard-nosed, yellow dog democrats living in Little Dixie right now. I know one guy who fought the civil war and the Republicans until the day he died. And afterwards probably.

* * * * * *

My grand father, Thomas C. Reynolds, on my mothers side, lived in Valliant, Oklahoma . He was one wild southern "yellow dog" democrat. He would hyperventilate if he found out that you were a "damn Republican or yankee" and was in his house. He might very well look you straight in the eye and firmly ask you to leave his domicile and "don't come back"! Then, in order to cleanse the air inside, he would stand erect and sing "Dixie" with his hand over his heart; and you had better stand, put your hand over your heart and sing right along, or you might be excused also.

Now, let me tell you what a kind and generous man my grandfather really was. He always made pretty good money even during the depression. He was the “pennant oil co” distributor in Choctaw and Mccurtain counties in the heart of Little Dixie. During week days he delivered gas and oil to a number of gasoline stations in the towns and through out the Quachita mountains. By the way, he would generally stop to fish at every creek he crossed, and also quite often he would park his truck on the road side and go deer or turkey hunting on his way back home.

On the week ends he did the normal things like go down and hangout at the gas station in town. The station was next to the wagon yard, on saturdays it would fill up with people trying to sell wagon loads of cookstove or fireplace wood. He was a soft touch for anyone who was really in trouble, so he would buy all the wood left in the wagon yard from the guys who had not sold their loads before time to go home.

I have seen his back yard, which was maybe 50 feet by 100 feet in size, almost completely covered with ricks of wood. There wasn’t enough room to walk between more than half of them. From time to time he would replenish what wood he used up for cooking or heating or when there was enough room to stack more. When he died, his back yard still had wood in it that had been there for years.

For years he had a pet tom turkey in his yard. It was a huge gobbler. It probably weighed 40 or more pounds. He was prouder of that turkey than anything, other than his family. He was an avid hunter and fisherman. I was fortunate enough to go hunting with him a few times. He told me that he didn’t really want to kill anything. He just wanted to go out in the woods for a while. He told me the main reason his family of 5 boys and 1 girl came to Indian territory was there were no hunting restrictions. They could hunt the year round. I suspect there were no bag limits to contend with either. I suppose he captured or found that little “tom” turkey somewhere on one of his “trips into the woods”.

He and that turkey were real friends. Whenever granddad was around him, the turkey would spread out his feathers and strut and walk in circles around him. “tom” would almost always “gobble” back when my grandfather “gobbled” at him. I know granddad and tom would talk “turkey”, when they were alone. When thanksgiving and christmas came each year, granddad would buy another turkey for our family’s holiday dinner. No one would even mention “tom” and certainly not the possibility of eating “you know who”!

“tom” always roosted in his little tree by the fence in the back yard. Every morning for years, granddad had gone to a window in the kitchen and checked on “tom”. One christmas eve morning, “tom” was gone. But apparently not by choice. Granddad went out immediately to find him. He found turkey feathers scattered around in the alley by tom’s tree. He spent the next few hours searching around the neighborhood trying to find him.

Just before noon, he found a few turkey feathers in a dear friends yard. His friend saw him looking around in his yard and asked him into his home. Then, he told my grandfather the whole truth. The man was having all his family for christmas dinner and had no money for food or presents for his little grandchildren. He had stolen old “tom” and was cooking him at that very moment. Both of those old men were broken hearted and wept when the reality of what had happened dawned on them..

Right then my grandfather went down town and bought several baskets of food and a bunch of little presents for his friend’s small grandchildren. He came back to their house, gave them the baskets, and wished them all a “very merry christmas". He told his friend that he would have given him any amount of money for their christmas if he only had asked.

Today a lot of politically correct people would ridicule him for his beliefs and prejudices. But I know there's one black family who would not.

* * * * * *

We lived in Boswell Oklahoma until I was about 4 years old. It is about 35 or 40 miles west of Valliant, still on the Frisco line. My father not only worked at the train station, he also ran the only hotel in town. As you would expect, my mother did most of the day to day work in the place. That left me without much supervision during the daytime. So, I had free run of the downtown area and the train station, which was only a block and a half away. I quickly became the town pest; but, everyone looked after my well being. In this particular case it did take a whole village to look after just one kid.

I kept the whole town in an uproar. I would get in the cars parked along the main highway in town and release the brakes and then I would "drive" it down the hill. One day the men were repairing the roof on our hotel. They had left the ladder leaning against the top of the 2—story hotel. I had climbed up the ladder to the top of the hotel and was walking around on the roof before I was caught.

As time went along, a girl child, Emily Jean, was born. A boy child, John Pascal, was then added to the family. My parents decided to get help for my mother to do the hotel work. There was just too much work for her. There was an elderly couple nearby that wanted the job. During the time we had been there, my mother had developed a close friendship with this couple and some of their children. His name, as you might guess, was "Uncle Tom" and hers was "Aunt Rachel". He was about 90 years old and she was 82 or 83. Both of them were in very good health. They would work every day all day long. Uncle Tom had been a slave back in the olden days.

Uncle Tom's main job was to take care of the outside and see that I was kept in check. Aunt Rachel helped my mother with the house work, and as the family grew, she took over some of the baby sitting job. Uncle Tom would work in our garden and I would trail along after him like a little puppy dog. He would tell me stories about his life as a slave on his masters farm. He would laugh about the little tricks he would play on "the massa", as he called him. Every once in a while his "massa" would lose his temper and give "Tom" a stinging shot with his beam flip. Uncle Tom recounted some of his early life. He said that slavery was a bad thing, but most of those he knew did about as well as every one else in the farm labor jobs. It was very had work. Some of the owners were mean to them and some were very good.

Occasionally, some of "Uncle Tom's" grand children, they might have been his great grandchildren, would come and visit with them a while. What better arrangement than let us kids play and entertain each other. He had one kid about the same age as I was. One day this kid asked me what I was doing. I happened to be sitting on the back step of the hotel working on my home made "slingshot". I told him that I was working on my "nigger shooter", that's what I had always called it. He quickly said, "dat ain't no nigger shooter, dat's a bean flip". So, guess what, we agreed to call it a bean flip. "Uncle Tom" had probably told him stories about the slavery days also.

Aunt Rachel had only one little sin. She smoked a little corn cob pipe. Well, so did my father smoke a pipe. When he was at home he would quite often fill his pipe with Prince Albert pipe tobacco. Aunt Rachel watched him like a hawk and when he did, she would get her pipe out and dad would fill hers also. She would then get down on the floor and pick up every flake of tobacco he dropped. She would say, "oh,Mr. Henry, let's not waste a drop of 'diss'. All 'diss' will come-handy later on."

I wish I could remember more about uncle Tom and aunt Rachel. We spent a lot of time together . He had told me a lot of stories about his life. Not many people can say they have heard the real and true accounts from that part of our history. I value that very much..

Sometime, I scared the "wadden out of everyone in town. I became the little kid on every block. Since we lived right in the middle of town, every merchant looked after me. They reported to my mother every thing I did, good or bad. I couldn't get a way with anything.

I got a new tricycle when I was about 3 or 4 years old. Most of the time I rode it right in the middle of the road through the middle of town as fast as it would go. The school house was on a hill about three blocks from the railroad station. I would take the tricycle to the very top of the hill, take my feet off the pedals, and let it fly down the hill at full speed. It would sail across the main street, which was a state highway, then on down another block or two then across the railroad tracks into a big ditch on the other side of the rails.

Generally some one in town would help me stop before I hit the rail yard or most of the time I would be able to stop before I hit the tracks. One time I was going so fast I couldn't get my feet back on the pedals and slow down. When I hit the first track, that tricycle's front wheel jumped higher than my head. I remember wondering what went with it. Then wham !— Man, I hit the sidewalk flat of my back! Sorry, that's the end of the story, I don't know what happened for a time after that!

I spent most of my spare time down at the railroad station where my father worked. I always wanted to ride in the engine cab while they were switching rail cars and tooting the train whistle. Quite often the engineers would stop the trains and lift me up into the engine cab and let me "drive" the train. They would tell me when I was supposed to blow the whistle. Man, that was the greatest thing in the world. I would pull on that dirty little cotton rope as hard as I could and she would holler as loud as she could.

I had a scrawny little cat that followed me everywhere I went. He and I would start touring the rail yard and end up a mile down the tracks. My mother told me, years later, that she was terrified every time she heard a train whistle coming into the station. She just knew they were "honking" at me and that cat. I think that may prove we may be overly concerned about the disappearance of the various endangered species we have on earth. We still have plenty of cats and kids.

Finally my father got "bumped" or maybe he "bumped someone else; anyway we ended up moving to Hugo Oklahoma . It was about 40 or 50 miles east of Boswell. He became the freight agent there. His biggest job, I think, was keeping records of the freight cars and their cargo that passed through . I remember that he would stand out on the station platform and record the car's identification numbers as the train left the station . He was the only man that I've heard about that could do that in real time. I know there was a lot of talk about that when he was there.

* * * * * *

When we moved to Hugo we were doing pretty well, in so far as making a living. We moved into a nice neighborhood. I was about 4 or 5 years old. Mother had another kid, shortly after we moved there. Another boy child, named Reynolds Ross, named after both of mothers families. All of us were getting big enough to learn how to ride tricycles, or learn to skate. We had a sidewalk in front of our house now, that speeded the learning process a little and increased the bumps and bruises.

I was totally surprised one day when my mother called me to "come in the house this very minute." I could tell she wasn't fooling around at all. I thought she was going to give me a spanking for something I had done. So instead of obeying her, I started running away from her by taking off around the house. All of a sudden she came charging out of the house like a wild bull. I ran inside the front door. I figured I could outrun her. So through the front door, through the kitchen, I was headed for the back door and freedom. When I got to the back porch, she was very close behind, so I gained all the speed I could. I hit the back door screen at warp speed!!. But! That damn thing was locked. Man, o man—- I bounced and staggered backwards a good 8 or 10 feet, right into her arms.

That's the first time I was totally out of it. I could see stars, lights going off and on and a lot of bells ringing! Well, she started laughing. That really did make me feel stupid and worthless. She laughed and laughed, laid down on the floor and laughed some more. After a while things settled down and I was ok. She said "the reason I called you, I was going to give you a piece of cake I just baked! Do you want it now, or do you want to go another lap around the house first"? And she started laughing again.

My mother was very firm in handling us kids. There were 3 or 4 of us by now and there was plenty of action around our house. Dad spent a lot of time at his job. Occasionally he would have to go to another station for a day or two and help someone catch up on their workload. That left mother with a lot of work just keeping things going. She was also the family disciplinarian when it was called for. Man, she didn't say "i'm going to tell your father about what you did! when he comes home, he will give you a good spanking". She took care of the problem right then and there by herself!

The rules of conduct were very clear. She had a set of rules that she said "you could keep living by". You did not tell her "I'm not going to do it". You could say "I don't want to do it" and hem haw around a little. But then you had better go do it. We did not sass her! or be sullen or defiant. We better not tell our parents a lie about anything. We dare not steal anything. The boys did not hit their little sisters or any other girl, even if they were beating the "stuffin" out of you. You didn't cheat, you didn't run from our parents when you were called. I had learned that the hard way. One of her rules was we had to share with each other. If one had something like a bar of candy, the owner would divide it, and the other guys could take first pick. You should see the amount of engineering measurements that it takes to divide a penny baby ruth candy bar equally.

One day she told me to get ready and dress, I had to start to school. It was just around the corner from our house. I really didn't know what she meant, but she got my good clothes out and I put them on. She took me out in the back yard and pointed me toward the school house. I was told to go and stay there until they let us out at lunch time. That's what I did. When I went into the school house, I had no idea what this was all about. But I went into the first room I came to. It just so happened to be the right one. The teacher told me to take a seat. She asked me my name and where I lived. I told her, and that was it. I was enrolled in school.

Some of the kids were crying to go back home. Some of them had their heads down on their desk, probably scared to death. We sang, "we are all in our places with sunshiny faces. Good morning dear teacher, good morning to you". The little girl that sat to my right was peeing in her pants and it was running down on the floor. I remember sitting there thinking, "I'm not going to like this."

I didn't have any trouble adapting to school. I had been playing down there a lot anyhow. I already knew how to seesaw and swing, real high, before I started to school.

The first thing we got into was practicing our penmanship i.e. Push— pulls and drawing rounded loop—t—loops. Things got wild shortly after we started. The teacher came by my desk and turned my sheet of paper around so it was slanting toward my left like all the other kids had theirs. When she left, I turned it back. Well, when she saw me do it she came back to my desk and turned my paper back like she had put it the first time and warned me not to change it. We then had a big "cuss fight", and I explained that I was left handed and the paper slanted my way kept me from having to write upside down and backwards. She looked at everything again ,smiled and said "ok, your way is better."

I guess financial conditions began to deteriorate at our house. We had to move out of the good side of town to the other side of the tracks, into 2nd ward school district. That one was in the tough side of town. I was approaching 7 years old, the age when kids begin to fight just for the fun of it. 2nd ward was the place in Hugo, Oklahoma where they had perfected after school fights into an art. Dad had bought me a pair of boxing gloves and a little sailors hat that had the words "i'm looking for the bully of the town" written around the brim. I practiced on my siblings with the gloves, but I didn't wear that damn stupid little hat outside of our yard. I was ready to go back to school. I hated to go to 2nd ward but I knew it was inevitable.

My mother kept adding rules to "keep alive by" as we grew older. The latest one was "you did not come home running from a fight with someone"; you stayed and fought. You might get whipped, that was ok, but you would get a bigger one later if you ran home and didn't fight the best you could. You did not start a fight, or jump on a kid smaller than you, but you could not run from anyone. You would be surprised how many fights you can avoid if you stand your ground and glare the other fellow down. Get right in his face, grit you teeth, slobber on your chin and growl real low at him that you are going to tear his face off if he touched you! But be prepared to fight in case it doesn't work!

My life in 2nd ward was not as bad as I had expected. Another kid was born. A girl, named Mozelle. That makes it 5 in all, 3 boys and 2 girls. When will it ever end?

* * * * * *

Little Dixie, like the rest of the nation, was approaching the depression period. It was relentless. We received a move order from the railroad. Dad was being transferred to Rogers, Arkansas. We knew nothing about Arkansas. It was just way up north. Dad had to go ahead of our moving. The work of packing fell on mothers shoulders. I was getting big enough to help her. I was the oldest and I got integrated into the family work force of 2, mother and I. I never was able to extract myself from that job until I graduated from high school and left home.

After mother and I got all our furniture and kids packed up ready for shipment, we all loaded on the train for the trip to Rogers. It was an all night trip. About an hour after we started the conductor came by to pickup our tickets. Of all things, mother had let the tickets get packed somewhere in our household goods. She could not produce them. The conductor got huffy and insisted she and all her kids would have to get off at the next stop.

My mother told him, in no uncertain terms, that was not going to happen! He kept pushing and insisting that she would have to get off. Well, she finally told him to go to hell and that if he touched her or one of her kids she would knock his damn brains out. He even threatened to disconnect the rail car she was in and set it on a side rail. She said "you go right ahead and make a fool out of your self if you want to! I'm not getting off". She, and all us kids rode into Rogers next morning on time. For better or worse, we were all still together. I think I was in the second and third grades at Rogers. I don't know whether Rogers was a happening city or whether life in Arkansas was a little more eventful than in Oklahoma . I began to get more involved in everything, both good and bad. I grew taller, but skinner, rather than the other way around. I remember that my folks decided I needed to gain a little weight, so they would buy a quart of milk each day, and I would get the cream off after it came to the top. It didn't help, but I sure did get to liking that cream. They stopped the practice but I didn't. I finally fell in with a bad companion, and we started stealing milk off the neighbors' porches where the milk man put it. It couldn't be wrong if we called it "white rabbit hunting", we got by with that a couple of nights; then, we got caught and you know what hit the fan! My net weight gain after the whole affair was "0".

I had been in school about two months, when I had my first fist fight on the school grounds. That always made it worse. The teachers would get involved and generally both guys got into trouble afterwards. This one started over a discussion of Easter. This other guy said there was no such thing as a rabbit that could lay an easter egg. I knew better because my dad and my mother both had told me there was ! We kept that argument up for a little while and then he got nasty and said my mother had told me a story. Well, that did it! I bopped him one on the nose. He started crying and several teachers started coming toward us and I should have taken off. But I wasn't smart enough to do it. I had to go to my teacher's room and explain the whole thing. I told her that he had started it. I told her the truth. He had said that rabbits could not lay easter eggs and I said they could.

We all enjoyed living in Rogers. It was a farming center for fruit and vegetable growing. It also had a bunch of "chinkey pin" trees. That's a real good nut that grew wild there. I think it was kin to the american chestnut which was killed out by a fungus that struck a few years later. Rogers was a good place to hunt and fish. It had a real good school system, so everything was ok.

There was a bunch of kids in our neighborhood who were into skating. The best sidewalk was on the other side of our street so we skated over there most of the time. It got to be a real mess, so much noise and talking and laughing that the neighbor on that side had the police come out to make us quit.

There were two old maids that lived there. I guess they were sorta cranky and surely didn't want a bunch of kids raising a fuss all the time. So it became a social problem. The police came over to our house and talked to my mother. They asked her to be sure that we did not get off the sidewalk onto their private property; but that the sidewalk was public property and the kids could skate all they wanted to on the other side of the street. Well, the word got out that these two old maids had complained about the noise, so a half dozen other kids started skating over there. After a few days our interest had changed and we started doing something else for fun.

As I look back, this was not like Little Dixie. Rogers was an older town. Their schools were built with brick, not wood. Their streets were paved. They had inside toilets and bathrooms. Little Dixie still had "outhouses" even in the nicer homes like my grandfathers. When he bought his last house, someone had just installed modern toilet facilities inside. Hell no!, My grandfather said, "there's not going to be any one using an "outhouse" inside his home. You had to go outside where god intended you should go. Ok to take a bath, but not the other". Everyone refused to obey this rule except him.

The new grade school in Rogers was very modern. It even had a fire escape from the top floor directly to the ground. It was a big metal tube that extend out through a trap door opening from the upstairs , down the outside of the building and opened up on the ground. The kids were supposed to jump inside the tube and slide all the way down to the ground.

Dad was taking John and me for a sunday morning walk one time. John was about two years old. He had great big eyes. The whole world was a wonder for John. He didn't talk until he was 3 or 4, other than to say "unda" and point to what interested him. I think the reason was that our little sister Emily Jean took care of everything he wanted and he had no reason to talk.

Dad said, "would you boys like to slide down that big fire escape?" I said "of course, yes we would". So he took us upstairs and found the little rubber door that opened into the tube. Then we planned every move very carefully. I would go first. Then dad would set John right next to the tube door, then dad would go. After he was out on the ground, he would call back up the tube for John to go. John would scoot over to the hole then he would shove off. It was a real exciting ride. First it was dark as night, then you could see the open bottom as it came at you like a shooting star. Then "zoom" and you were there and on the ground!

Well, dad came down. Then he gave John the ok. There was a few seconds delay. I guess John was deciding if he really wanted to go so soon. After a few moments we heard him coming down the tube. As he came into view, he looked like two giant eyes, straddling a giant open mouth as he came out the bottom of that pipe. Dad caught him at the bottom and John was speechless. When we got through laughing and as we turned away to leave, John turned around pointed to the opening and said "unda"!

While we were living there, two historical events took place. We had bought a new Atwater-Kent radio. It was the model that had the big speaker phone sitting on top of the radio. Then on Oct. 21, 1931 the famous inventor Thomas Alva Edison died. After the funeral, President Hoover spoke to the nation to honor Mr. Edison. After he had finished, there would be one minute of silence and all lights in the nation would be cut off to show respect for mr. Edison and show the contrast with the way it was before he invented the light bulb. This event took place a couple of years after the 50th anniversary of the invention of the light bulb. Mother made all of us kids listen to him talk. She told us that Mr. Edison was a world famous man and that we should listen to what he said.

The other event was a dirigible that was making a flight around the world and they were going to broadcast a live radio message from it as it flew over some city in the east. They were going to make the broadcast from inside of the dirigible. High tech wasn't just invented you know. They did and we listened.

Our parents were very careful that we kids became aware of the good and important things that were going on in the world. When a President spoke on radio, even before President Roosevelt made his fireside chats famous, we had to listen when a President spoke. Especially if he was a democrat. Little Dixie was not far away and our granddad might be watching.

* * * * * *

We didn't stay in Rogers very long, about a year. Dad got his notice to move back to Hugo and we immediately started packing. Again, he had to go ahead of the move. That left mother and me to pack and take care of all the moving chores. I had to tell my teacher that I was leaving. I started gathering up my books and pencils and other stuff. She came over and helped me . When I started out of the room, she followed me to the door that went outside. She went with me onto the little stoop just outside the door. As I turned to wave "good bye" she stooped over and hugged me and kissed me on the forehead. She muttered something like, if I ever came back, she wanted me to be in her class. Lordy, even though it was cold outside, I got so hot, hot, hot. It was such a surprise I didn't know what to say or do. I had always thought that maybe I was her pet. I think she was the same teacher that I had to explain the fight I had about the easter bunnies that could lay easter eggs.

Back to Hugo! This time mother had her train tickets in her purse so we had no trouble with the conductor. This move was just before Christmas. It was very cold. The temperature, in Rogers when we left, was around 10 below zero. We moved into a little shot- gun house out at the east edge of Hugo. Even in Hugo everything outside was frozen. I found a little cotton tail rabbit in our barn that had frozen to the ground and he could not run away. I worked him loose and took him in the house and warmed him up. He got ok.

The depression was taking hold. More and more people were losing their jobs and homes. Dad was lucky to have any job. He still worked full time, but I think some of it was on the "extra board". That is a list of guys that filled in for vacations, sick spells and otherwise part time work. I know my parents talked about it from time to time.

The reality of hard times caused my folks to buy a cow. We had about 10 or 12 acres for pasture and a garden. I was the one who had to learn to milk and take care of that cow. It wasn't too bad for a while, but every night and every morning, 7 days a week, 4.3 weeks per month, 12 months a year, I had to be there on time and milk that damn cow. It made no difference whether it was rain, shine, sleet, snow, tornadoes and lightening. There are 3 things that are certain in this world. They are death, taxes and milking cows. But it sure helped feed all us kids.

By the way, we had another boy child shortly after we moved to Hugo, Oklahoma . His name was Jerry Drew. He was named for I don't know who. This was the first time that my parents didn't use an old family name.

For me , it was back to the 1st ward school district. That is where I started to school, but this time it had taken on the characteristic of being tough to get to and from school every day without a fight. I had to go down an old woodsy country road for about I mile, then about a half mile down a state highway. About the 2nd or 3rd day we walked home, I noticed 3 or 4 little Indian kids that used the same road.

I found out that they were the Simpson children they lived about a quarter of a mile further out of town than we did. There was another kid or two that I saw only once in a while making the same trip. The Simpsons had two Indian boys about my size and an Indian girl. She was much bigger than me. This was not good news back in those days when fighting was a universal sport.

My little sister, Emily Jean, was one of the kids that walked to and from school with me in the same crowd. I felt that, sooner or later, we were going to have trouble with one of the Simpson tribe. I had an old baseball that I took to school to play with. I saw one of them looking at it with a lot of interest. We would throw it back and forth to one another as we came home. One afternoon on the way home it happened. I threw it to one of the Simpson kids and he would not let me have it back. As I would get near to him, he would throw it to another. I finally got it, but suddenly the girl grabbed me from behind. Then one of her brothers started trying to take the ball away from me and hitting me in the face. I jammed my elbow in her stomach and kicked the kid that was in front of me. They all quit fighting me and started trotting and running ahead, crying and threatening to tell my mother on me.

When I got home. I started to tell my mother what had happened. While I was busy telling her, about that time the phone rang. It was Mrs.. Simpson on the war path, speaking about half english and the rest in choctaw. She was threatening my mother. She told mother she was coming down to the house and see that I was punished. You know mothers, especially mine, she was a hot head and would not take a threat like that at all. She told Mrs.. Simpson to come on down but be ready to fight because she was ready; and mother assured her that someone would have to carry her back home. Well, then Mrs.

Simpson started hedging her threat to the point that she postponed the match until after she got supper for her kids. She never did show.

That was ok at our house. So the whole thing blew over. As time went on, of course, we kids forgot about it and started playing with each other again. Her kids came down to our house , we went up to theirs. Pretty soon Mrs. Simpson sent her kids to borrow something like baking soda or flour . Mother started neighboring with her. As time went on, mother called Mrs. Simpson for something, and everything was forgiven. We all became really good friends.

Mother and Mrs. Simpson started visiting each other nearly every day, talking about things that were happening in the neighborhood. Mother later asked me what actually happened that day. I told her and she said, "see, I told you that things would turn out ok if you did not run from a fight. You did the right thing. Do you still have your baseball?" And I said, "yes I do".

One of the Simpson kids was the first to tell me about the Indians "Happy Hunting Ground" . That's where they will all go when they die. He said that place is a beautiful forest, pretty rivers, plenty of game to hunt and fish to catch and they will live there forever in peace and happiness around their own camp fire. I guess their father might have gone there. We never did see a Mr. Simpson.

Little Dixie was getting poorer and poorer. Working wages were dropping. As a kid I depended on grown up talk to learn what was happening. We were reasonably well off. Dad was still working. We still had the Atwater Kent radio so we could keep up with what news there was.

There were about 4 or 5 rabbit traps left by the previous residents that lived in our house. Dad got them out and showed us how to set them. John was getting big enough to help me run the traps every evening. At first we actually ran them every few hours. It was exciting. When we caught a rabbit, mother would dress it and we would have gravy and biscuits and a big platter of golden fried rabbit. We did eat good , but money became harder and harder to get.

John and I even hired out to pick cotton to help them. Mother fixed us a little cloth sack with a strap on it to put around our shoulder. We used it to put the cotton in. The cotton farmer nearby agreed that we could help them pick. The first day mother fixed us a big breakfast and we started out as part of Americas work force. We had plans of buying mother a new dress and I was going to get a left handers baseball glove. John was going to help.

The first day on the job we left at 5 o'clock in the morning, still dark. We worked like the devil. We wanted to get it all picked before noon. By 10:00 0'clock, we were bushed , our hands were sore, we figured we had enough cotton to buy everything we needed; so we weighed our sack in and went home. The farmer paid everyone on the following friday afternoon. We could hardly wait until payday. Finally our paycheck came. It was a check for the total amount of 2 cents each! The depression had hit us real hard and it hurt! Every fall after harvest time there was a traveling circus or carnival that came to town the one that came to Hugo that year was a good big circus. I think you judge their size by the number of "rings" that entertain simultaneously. This one had 3 rings. It had a large herd of elephants and camels and wagons with all sorts of animals.

This was the top event of the year. Of course I could go to see it after school. Just don't stay out too late. That was my mothers instructions for the day. After school I ran all the way to the circus grounds. It was in an area of town that I was not familiar with, but I was sure I could find my way home even after dark. Of course I didn't have any money. I could have a good time without money.

It was a joyous experience. I spent all afternoon just looking at the free activities. Every little side show would put on a sample of what was inside. This was great. All during this time I was planning, or rather I was scheming how I could slip into the circus. I had some experience with that before. However I didn't have a very good record of success. But it was worth a try. Actually, dark came up on me before I noticed. They started turning the night lights on, cars were driving up with their lights on, parking all over the place and in different directions.

I must admit , by dark I had no idea which way my home was. I couldn't even recall which road that I used to come into the circus grounds. I was in deep do-do- as the grown ups say. They had turned on the big outside lights for the circus tent. Street lights had been turned on. It wasn't the same place I had come into that afternoon. By dark, I was hungry squared. Not one red cent did I have. I didn't know which way to get home.

I had laid my plans before dark on how to slip into the big top! At least I was going to be able to see the show. But, by the time the show started, the circus acts had lined up at every exit all over the outside of the tent. They would go in and parade around. I couldn't even find the spot I had planned to go under the tent flap. I tried one I thought was it and it turned out to be right where the elephants were parked, my plan had been shot to hell! I would look around to orient myself to go home and couldn't even do that. Plan "B" came to be to wait until the show was over then I could follow the line of cars into town. I could find my way home from there.

I was really worried about not doing what my mother told me to do. "don't stay late". It was a long, long time before the show was finished. But at least I was going to be able to go home. But no, plan "B" didn't work either. Instead of a line of cars going back to town, there was a dozen lines going in all directions. Finally, I was left there almost alone, except for the workers that started taking the tents and everything down. I was one frustrated kid. It must be close to midnight.

Finally I started in the direction I thought was most probably the way home. I would walk in that direction for a while, then I would reevaluate. I did that 3 or 4 times. Then I began to see things that looked familiar like a tree or a house or a road corner. That was the darkest damn night I had ever experienced. Not one speck of light anywhere. After a long time of wandering, I found myself. I was on an old wagon road running through the woods. I had used it one time for a short cut to town.

It was so dark I had only the outlines of the trees against the sky to guide me. But I had found where I was. I was less than a half mile from home. Boy, did I scoot along the rest of the way. When I got there, my parents were still up. They said nothing about being upset with me for disobeying them. They were really concerned about me. I told them my story. They listened carefully. When I finished, dad said, "oh, we knew you could find your way back." Then I went to bed completely exhausted, but one happy kid.

* * * * * *

There were two things that started occupying my thoughts from time to time. They were about what I was going to do when I grew up. That seemed to be the question that all grown ups want you to answer. My first choice was to fly an airplane. That seemed to me to be the greatest thing on earth. Aviation was in it's infancy. Our radio would occasionally cover some aviation event that just set me on fire. That was it! I would occassionally read a pulp magazine that had a world war 1 airplane story in it. The idea of flying a fighter plane in combat was my choice. I just knew I could do it better than anyone else could; so that was my answer to "what are you going to be when you grow up" question!

The other possibility was to be a baseball player. I was left-handed and I thought that gave me a leg up on a right handed pitcher. I know my father did also. He had played baseball in the old, old Texas league. He supported me in that choice also.

The only problem I had was that I never had a left-handers glove in my life. I always had to use a right-handers glove. Of course it never fit. Then one sunday morning I was down town. I saw a used left-handers glove in the show window of the only pawn shop in town. The store was closed! My god, it was about two miles home. I ran every step of the way. I told my dad what I had found. I thought, depression or no depression I had to have that glove. My dad agreed, bless his sweet soul. I could go get it monday morning, no matter how much it cost, [up to a dollar.] That glove was going to be mine.

Monday morning I finally got down town around 9 o' clock. The store had been open about an hour. The glove was gone! What the hell, I wasn't too upset, I was going to fly airplanes anyhow! But damn! I wanted that glove.

Well, it happened again. Somewhere along about this time mother had another one, a little girl, named Mozelle, after my mothers's younger sister. That put our family at 5 kids. 3 boys and 2 girls. Jean was the big sister now. She was so proud to have a little sister. She had been contending with that bunch of boys alone. Don't let anyone tell you that boys and girls are not different. However, my mother did contend as well, that there was no difference in little boys and little monkeys.

Later in life our family had the opportunity to visit the zoo in Oklahoma City. We went to the big monkey island exhibit there. Mother watched the monkeys play with their toys, running in and around the trees and along the moats edge. Finally she said, "my God, I can believe every word that Darwin said about evolution in his writings. I can recognize characteristics in every one of my kids that match that bunch of devilish little monkeys!"

The relentless pressure of the depression just wouldn't go away. Dad worked less and less. It had gotten to the point that he decided he was going to lose his job, sooner or later, and that he would be forced to do something besides railroading. There was no work anywhere. Guys who were hunting work of any kind started coming by our house and asking for something to eat. They would do anything for a meal. Cut some wood for our stove, work in the garden, fix fence, just about anything. Mother never turned them down. She always had enough cooked to give them a good meal and didn't ask them to do any work. No one ever offered to milk those damn cows! That was still my job.

Dad finally rented a big farm place 4 miles out on the other side of town. It was a fairly large farm, 180 acres, about 60 in cultivation and the rest in pasture and forest. We could raise a few animals to sell or to eat. There was nice big timber growing there. We could keep warm by cutting our own wood and also raise food for our family and our animals so that's what we did.

We moved out on the farm, but dad still worked once in a while on the "extra board". This was not a bad situation. He got enough cash together to buy another cow now and then, a horse or a team of mules and a wagon. So off we go .

The farm house we rented was a large three bedroom, no inside bathroom , no central heat, except one fireplace in the living room. A wood cook stove in the kitchen. No running water. We had a cistern to catch rainwater in the back yard. You went outside to get water. Now, don't turn your nose up at this, it was a nice up to date farm house. It was big enough for our family of 7 . We were much better off than most everyone in the area.

Getting food and wood in for the winter was the first priority. Dad still had his old army 45 pistol from world war1. He traded that for a barrel of sorghum molasses, a sow pig that was about to have piglets and $ 5.00 cash. He and I started cutting cook stove and fireplace wood. We soon had plenty of wood to last all winter. Cold weather was coming and at least we could eat and keep warm. That was better than a lot of people in the cities . The government was putting up soup kitchens all over the nation around the big industrial areas. There was no welfare assistance or unemployment checks. At that time, when you lost your job, you started starving that day.

This depression thing really was serious. There was no class or color distinction. It hit everyone! People were jumping out of windows in the big banks in New York. They were committing suicide all over the place. Banks were going broke. This was still a year or two before it "peaked" with the "bank holiday", later declared by President Roosevelt. Hoover was still president. This was the thing that killed the republicans, at least in Little Dixie. They were trying to get Hoover to spend some money, but he refused to do any deficit spending. I'm sure that wasn't the whole cause of the great depression, but that's the cause that stuck in the minds of the people where I lived.

Dad was working enough and trading a little, this for that. Pretty soon we had 12 or 14 half wild half starved cows. 3 or 4 horses and a team of mules and some old farm equipment. But no money!

Mother started raising chickens. If you ever go broke, start raising chickens, they are always in demand. You could always sell a chicken when you couldn't sell anything else. We kids would shell peanuts or corn on the halves, for the farmers that had raised them the year before. Our neighbors would give us potatoes, corn for meal and other staples that helped us through the first winter. Everyone helped everyone else, regardless of station in life. That was one of the good things about the depression. You had no governmental help of any kind. We turned to each other for help. We survived!

Attending school presented some problems. We lived about a mile or so from the only school in the district. The only school around was the Goodland Indian School. It was a private school run by the Presbyterian church for Indians and we wern't Indians. After some negotiations, dad made arrangements for his kids. He arranged for me , Jean and John and 2 or 3 kids in another family near us, to send their kids to Goodland. We had to walk the two miles every day. There was no school bus to pick us up. My sister Emily Jean and our brother John and I were finally enrolled in school. There were the 2 other kids, our neighbor's two little girls, about the same age as we were.

Our first days in school were no different than elsewhere. As time went on we noticed that we were not making any new friends. No one bothered us but no one offered to be our friend. Those little Indian kids were very aloft. As it turned out, and as we better understood their ways, they just don't talk very much, and they didn't make new friends worth a hoot. They were just not interested in us. We were the ones that were different. They had a knack of looking at you and seeing right through you. Quite often we would be out for recess and you could feel some one present, but not there. Keep looking around, there would be someone near by, around the corner or from behind a tree, looking right at you. When you smiled or noticed him, he would leave. After a few weeks, things began to change.

The class room contacts became more relaxed and friendly. They began to talk to us a little and then they would smile if you smiled at them. We were finally becoming part of their world. Soon, we were playing their games and they started conversations with us. We started playing games like "tops" and "marbles" with them. Finally they accepted us fully.

The only place where we didn't fit in was in their sports like football and baseball. They pretty much kept us at arms length. However we couldn't join them anyhow. We had to start home immediately after school. We always had to get home before dark. I still had to milk 6 or 7 old half dry cows and help with the other chores around the house and barn every night late and every morning early! Damn that depression.

The schools we had been going to did not have football. But the Goodland Indian school did have it and they knew how to play it. They played with all the spirit and energy a kid could have. Most of them were rather short, stocky and stout as a little bull.

I feel they were inspired by the great Oklahoma Indian football player and olympic star, Jim Thorpe. I,m not sure of that, but something was sure inspiring them. If he was active at that time I am sure he was their hero and inspiration as well as a great role model for them.

Their game could be anywhere, in the school yard, in a cow pasture, in a brushy field with rocks and cow flaps, they played anywhere. It didn't matter. They played bareheaded and most of the time they were barefooted and bare knuckled. I'm glad they did not invite me to play. It was much too rough and violent for me.

Farming was not a good career field for me. I had to join the ranks of the grown men and go to the field every day just like they did. This isn't the way to learn to fly an airplane! Dad would hire someone to help when he could afford it or when he happened to get a little pay for extra board assignment and would be gone for a few days. I won't try to describe the routine a farmer has, but the day started badly, especially when you had to milk a half dozen old dry range cows at 4 am just to get a gallon or two of milk.

From time to time dad and I would take a rick of stove wood to town on saturday and he would stay in the wagon yard until we sold it for $.75 a rick. There were times when we got caught at sundown, and still had not sold our wood.

Late one afternoon, we were still there when it started getting dark. Some religious group was having a revival in a big tent they had set up in the wagon yard. So about dark, they rolled up the tent flaps and started holding their services. Naturally I was hanging around on the outside watching this development when suddenly a little fellow, at least a foot shorter than I was, walked up to me and said, "I can whoop you". Man! That was a surprise and I wasn't ready for an encounter like that. I just ignored him for a little while, shortly I felt him tug on my overalls pocket, "hey, did you hear me?" He repeated, "I can whoop you, and if you will come out here in the wagon yard i'll show you I can!"

By this time the lights in the tent were all on and it had turned darker outside. I never did claim to be a fighter, but I wasn't going to let this little bastard bully me around, I was still a foot taller than he was. "Ok", I said, "lets go". He started out away from the tent, so I followed . He had walked about 6 or 8 feet out of the tent flap light into the dark, when he suddenly turned like a snake and hit me right in the eye, with his hard little fist! I went blind as a bat in that eye. I couldn't see even out of the other one. I heard him yell, "see I told you!"— Then he was gone. I finally got a little sight back in both eyes. I looked that wagon yard over and over and couldn't find that little bastard anywhere.

On the way back home that night, dad and I were setting on the spring seat in the wagon. We were talking about what I had learned about defending myself, when suddenly he started laughing at my story. Then we both got to laughing about me getting suckered in on that one. My eye had swollen shut, I guess he could visualize how funny I must look even in the dark.

* * * * * *

As it is said , into each life some rain must fall. There is also a saying, if there's a drought, a little rain may save your farm. That's what the soldier's bonus did in 1933, I know that the senate rejected it in 1932. It may have saved our family and farm. Dad had served in France during WW1 for a good long time, most of it in combat. Dad's bonus was a little over $550.00. My god, that was a fortune during the depression ! That was more clear profit than we would make in 2 years farming. It came out of the blue. What joy and relief and gratitude! We were rich !

My mother, who had been working for years in a hot kitchen with a bunch of little kids hanging on her dress tail, crying or yelling mamma, mamma a 1000 times a day, and begging for the lord only knows what, was saved by that bonus I think, from an early death. Every year she made a big garden, raised over 200 chickens, maybe had a new kid. She canned over 500 jars of food from her garden. She took care of all of us, she cooked and washed a bunch of dishes 3 times a day. She carried in her water from the water cistern and cleaned the house. Fed every living thing on the farm except the live stock, she did the washing on a rub board and hung it out to dry, I started helping her when I was 10 or 11 years old. I never went to school on mondays after that. But she would not sew or iron, so we wore it wrinkled with holes and no buttons.

Dad was working night and day on either the extra board or in the field. I was milking 10 or 12 sorry old mean range cows every morning and night, rain or shine. Hell, I was only about 10 or 12 years old! I tell you farming is no damn good, especially when you are yearning to fly like a "bird".

Dad would take a 10 gallon cream can full of thick sweet cream down town to the ice cream factory and they wouldn't give him over 2 or 3 dollars for it. He started bringing it back home and feeding it to the hogs. We all agreed that it was better to give it to our hogs than to the creamery downtown. A 100 lbs. sack of beautiful irish potatoes would not sell for 50 cents, delivered to your door step. At times, you couldn't sell a dozen eggs for 5 cents! One thing about it you could always sell an old hen that weighed around 8 lbs for $.20 or $.25, maybe 30 cents. That was our only cash crop. It's no wonder that stealing chickens was one of the most lucrative career fields at that time.

The soldiers bonus was the thing that inspired enough hope and ambition in my parents to keep trying. They had 5 kids at that time, 3 boys and two girls. Dad and mother called us all together and told us of the good fortune. We were all so excited; especially when they told us that we would all take a bath, get dressed up, get in the wagon and go to town. Each one of us could pick out any one thing we wanted really badly and they would buy it for us. That started a lot of yelling and jumping up and down and running through the house hunting the Sears Roebuck catalogue, but it was out in the "you know what".

When the check came, we all took a bath, put on our best clean cloths, got in the wagon and away we went to downtown Hugo. I wanted a pair of high top lace—up leather boots that had a pocket knife in a little scabbard on the side of the boot. I think John wanted a b-b gun. As I remember, Jean wanted a bilow doll, it would close it's eyes when you laid it down on its back. Mother was going to get some winter cloths for the kids and may get herself a new dress. Dad didn't want anything as I remember. He must have been happy with the joy he saw as he watched all the kids and mother happy, healthy, and having such a good time at last. Just think, $550.00!

We all had soda pops and hamburgers for lunch. There was candy for all. This orgy went on all day. We finally piled in the wagon late in the afternoon and started home. By the time we got home, it was well after sundown, all the kids had fallen asleep, scattered all over that wagon. We were worn out, but full of hamburgers, soda pop and candy. We each had our most prized, new belongings near by. I know that our mother and dad must have been supremely happy. All their kids were healthy and happy. They must have felt a tremendous amount of joy and relief from the grind of poverty for the first time in years.

Our trip , with all the things we bought and ate, cost much less than $50.00. For us, things began to improve. But for my dad farming was not his thing. As I look back, I feel that this event gave him inspiration to look for something better. He had always worked with numbers, schedules, rules and regulations. While he was with the railroad, he had developed his own methods and the ability to work with numbers. He could add a long column of 5 and 6 digit numbers before you could get your pencil and paper. He had only finished the 5th grade in school. He helped us with our math all during school. The only problem was, he could not tell us how he managed to get such quick answers.

He was adamant that every one of his kids was going to get a college education. You must consider what unusal foresight that was back then, at that time no one in his family had even finished high school. My mothers family was doing ok with high school. Mother had graduated from high school and had taught school up in the Quachita mountains for a couple of years. But no one had ever been to college. Both of our parents laid the law down with emphasis, we had to go to college. We could work our way through. They would help when they could, but the shortage of money was no excuse!

* * * * * *

They decided that we needed to move to a place where they had a chance to do better. Mothers family lived in Valliant, it was only 30 miles away. Her father was influential there, he may could help dad get a job. I was finishing the 5th grade in Goodland. There was no high school at Goodland, so they would eventually have to make new arrangements for high school somewhere. Jean and John were strung out in the lower grades. Reynolds was too young for school. So we started packing and getting ready to move. We sold as much of our equipment and farm supplies as we could. That income helped a little, but we were left with 4 or 5 horses, 6 or 8 cows and calves. I still had my personel horse, "Ben",I wouldn't sell him for any amount.

In my opinion "Ben" was an unusual horse. He wasn't very big, but his confirmation and attitude were magnificent. He walked and ran with his head high and his ears standing straight up pointed straight ahead. He kept his neck bowed and his chin pulled back. He was a prancer and was "on stage" all the time. He had one bad habit I could never understand, nor retrain him from. I could not tie his head to anything, such as tying his reins to a rail. He would go crazy, and would likely injury himself if I didn't untie him. I would ride him and when I got off him I would put his reins on the ground and he never would leave that spot. If I had to tie him, I would wrap a little rope around his ankle and he would not make a single objection or leave that spot. Ben was 21 years old.

Mothers family had recently bought and moved into a real nice home in Valliant. Their old house was vacant. They said we could have that place. If we wanted to move to Valliant.

Grandmothers family was almost grown. Her youngest of 6 children was my age. I know that their grown family did not look forward to having a bunch of grand children around all the time. But they were wonderful. We all fit in just fine. The more the merrier !

Our family had always gone to grand mothers house to have the biggest christmas dinner you ever saw and to celebrate christmas day. They always had a great big christmas tree and we all exchanged gifts like crazy. That was considered the biggest party of the year in our family.

When we were very young and were getting ready to go to grandmothers house for christmas, dad would build a little platform on the back floor of our car. It would be level with the back seat. Mother would spread quilts and blankets in the back seat so we could keep warm. Our journey to grandmothers house was never more that 30 or 40 miles, but it was on a dirt road scarred with wagon wheel ruts frozen in the mud and in many cases, covered over with snow and frozen rain. Some time it would take a couple of hours to make the trip. Maybe longer if we had more than one or two flats.

At that time cars did not have heaters in them, so dad would light a coleman lantern and put it in the floor board of the front seat to warm their feet. The kids were all snug and warm under blankets in the back seat. We called that arrangement a "suv" "sports/ utility vehicle" configuration, I don't know what they would call it now. [I just madeup the "suv" part of this story.]

* * * * * *

Now, my parents decided that moving was an improvement for dad's chance at getting work. We were going to make the trip to grandmothers house a permanent arrangement. We are moving lock, stock and barrel to Valliant. More correctly, we were moving wagon, stock and all our junk. We were sure our grandparents would still welcome us as if it were a christmas day.

Our trip from Hugo to Valliant was the reverse of the story of "the grapes of wrath." We moved east and those folks moved west. They had cars. We had a wagon load of useless junk. We had tied our extra horses and a cow or two to the wagon and was leading them along highway 7o east out of Hugo. Dad was driving the wagon, I was riding old "Ben". Mother and the kids had gone ahead in granddads flat bed oil truck. Her brother had came to Hugo and taken everyone and everything they could carry back to Valliant the day before.

Dad and I left the farm just at daylight. In an hour or so we went through Hugo with all that mess still hanging together. If we could make it through Hugo, we figured we could make it to Valliant. We bought a big chunk of rat cheese and a box of crackers.to eat along the road. The great migration was under way!

Driving a herd of live stock tied to a wagon was not a hard thing to do. Once in a while I would stick a big toe in a cows ribs to wake her up. But no great problems came up early on. We figured we were averaging nearly 2 miles per hour. That would put us in Valliant about dark. Not bad.

Dad wondered out loud if he could even stop that contraption without some of the live stock getting tangled up and panicking. Maybe trying to stop would not be nearly as bad as trying to turn them all at a corner. Fortunately, it was almost a straight shot to Valliant. There were a few long gradual curves, but probably everybody would follow ok.

After a few hours of highspeed cruising after we left Hugo, we stopped in the shade for a little rest Traffic was not going to be a problem. I don't think there was a half dozen cars or wagons on that highway all day long. After a short rest, he asked me if I would like to ride in the wagon a while. I certainly would. Bareback riding is not really a great way to get anywhere. The problem was, I could not tie my horse, Ben, to the wagon. He had this mental problem with being tied to anything. He would panic and start bucking and cutting up. He would go crazy. We sure didn't want that. So we finally decided to let him just follow along behind the wagon without restraints. I knew old Ben really well. We had been together for a good long time. So, that's what I did. I tied his reins up on his back and got up in the wagon seat. I looked back at Ben and told him to come on and he immediately started walking right behind that wagon and never once did he get out of position or lag behind. It's no wonder I still love that faithful and loyal friend.

This trip was made sometime during july or august. It was hot and dry. We had brought a barrel of water for the stock, but we began to run low earlier that we planned. About late lunch time we stopped at a farm house along the road and asked if we could water our stock from his well. The farmer hesitated and started making excuses. His well was low, our stock may have some disease that would infect his stock. We knew he was not going to let us. So dad thanked him and we started up again. Our main reaction was that we were surprised that he refused us. Everyone else had been so nice.

When we got to Sawyer, Oklahoma , the man that had a service station there let us draw water from his well and we managed to satisfy all our stock with cool, clear, well water. We ate cheese again and had some cool, clear, well water for ourselves.

I decided to get back on Ben and ride him a while. That hardwood wagon seat wasn't much better riding than being bare back.

We must have looked like a wagon loaded with junk, headed for a disposal site. We had plows on board, some little buckets and big buckets, some big boxes tied on, a barrel or two inside, rope holding it all together. We had a few bales of hay to feed the stock on the way. A crate or two of chickens setting on top of it all. I remember we had a bedstead leaning over the side. We put it on the side where the ditch would be.

We weren't having any real trouble. It was tiring and hot. Some of the stock would get a little cranky at times. On and on we went. I started switching more often from my horse to the wagon seat. Dad and I would talk from time to time about going fishing and hunting when we could go up in the mountains north of Valliant. We would eat a little more cheese and drink a lot of water. We were never bored. Tired yes, but not bored. That was a very good day I spent with my father.

We made it to Swink, Oklahoma , 6 miles from Valliant at about 5 or 6 o'clock in the afternoon. We didn't want to be on the highway after dark. We didn't have a single light on the wagon or anywhere in our crowd. We were a menace on the road. So we tried to speed everyone up a little, it worked for a little while. We started moving a bit faster. Clear creek zipped by at about 2.01 miles and hour. Then the graveyard about 7 o'clock. It was a little less than 2 miles from Valliant. We crossed the railroad track in Valliant just before dark. We were only six blocks from home!

We finally had to make a sharp turn to the left then back to the right. It was smooth, smooth. Every cow and horse we had made it without any fuss. Ben held his position just perfectly. We pulled up in the front yard of our new home right on time. Dad took all the livestock to our barn. He fed and watered them. Shortly he came back and mother had fixed a great supper of fried chicken, hot biscuits and milk gravy. We were all back in our places with sun shiny faces!

It wasn't a very long time, we hadn't unpacked completely, when mother sent all us kids to spend the night at grandmothers house. When we got back home the next day we had a new little brother. We named him Walter Cleveland Gardner after mother's uncle Walt, who had the service station in town. That made 5 boys and 2 girls, not bad for the depression years. It proves that money isn't everything. We were as happy a family as anyone could have, even if we had been rich. Mother had said that the first thing she looked for when a new child was born, was it ok and all there. If it was, she was happy with it.

The story goes that some of mother's friends were telling a neighborhood joke about a priest having congratulated my parents on their fine catholic family. My mother answered by saying "oh, no we aren't catholic, just passionate protestants".

Dad immediately went to work at the service station. We had brought a few of our chickens on the wagon and cashed them in as we needed a little money. We had brought what cow feed we had, so everything got started off ok. Dad sold two or three of the horses right away. I could keep old Ben. But I still had to milk those damned old cows.

* * * * * *

We had very little adjusting at our new home, it was where we had always visited our grandmother. September wasn't very far away and that means going back to school. I would be in the 6th grade when I started at Valliant. I had been in school about a month when I went to a school program in the school auditorium one night.

All of a sudden, someone touched me on the shoulder and handed me a note. It said, "I will meet you in the parking lot after this is over. Stop trying to steal my girl". It wasn't signed. If it had been I wouldn't have known who it was. I glanced around to see if anyone was watching me. I noticed one guy about 3 or 4 rows back and to my left. He snarled at me and showed me his fist.

I had been hoping that I wouldn't have to fight my way into Valliant school. But apparently I was wrong. Here I go, it happens every time I moved into a new neighborhood. I had no one with me. I was vulnerable without some one to help me if they ganged up on me. There was nothing I could do but meet the bastard. I would glance over at him once in a while. He was tall and skinny like me. I could whip his ass, I figured, but I hated to start off in a new school this way. Even if I whip him, I'll have to take on the next guy up the pecking order.

After the program, I went out the door and headed for the parking lot. Hell, there was a ring of boys that had formed a big circle, before I got half way out there. I walked up and they made a little path for me. I walked inside the circle and stopped. There, standing on the inside, was this guy I had seen during the program. He was grinding his fist around and around like he was warming up. He asked my name. I told him and I asked what his name was. He told me it was "Jack" something. I said 'what do you want with me'? He said "you have been trying to steal my girlfriend". "I don't know your girlfriend and I haven' been trying to steal anyone's girl friend" I answered.

By this time I knew that there was no way out and he started to bad mouth me again. We had moved up fairly close to each other. So I stepped up and just hauled back and hit him right on his big bony nose. The blood shot out of it and he went to the ground flat as a flitter. He was down there trying to get up and trying to make it stop bleeding. Blood was all over his face and his upper body. I had hit him as hard as I could. He started trying to crawfish out of the fight. He said he was just kidding and trying to see if I was a coward or would I fight. I took a look around the circle a couple of times. I would ask a complete stranger, "do you want to take me on? The answers I got all the way around was no! They opened up a little path and I walked out. Unfortunately "Jack" was just the stalking horse for the town jock. I would meet him later on. I was rising to the top of the pecking order very fast.

All of mothers siblings had lived in Valliant all their lives and had graduated from Valliant high, so we were very well known . I played baseball and other sports. My horse Ben was the fastest horse in town. That raised my statue. As time went on our house became the community center for most the kids our size in town, and we had them all sizes. It wasn't unusual for 15 or 20 kids to be playing at our house at one time. Mother played the piano and dad played the fiddle. They would let the kids dance at our house and they had as much fun as anyone. There would be kids dancing and there would also be 3 or 4 tables of dominos or card games going on at the same time.

A few of the older boys started bringing chickens to our house. They had "found" them lost around their house. They wanted mother to cook them at our impromptu parties. She would start frying those "lost" chickens late in the evening and by 9 0r 10 o' clock we would all have a big hot supper of fried chicken , milk gravy, biscuits and fried potatoes. I've seen her fry as many as 9 chickens of all sizes. She would have a dishpan full of fried chicken and over a gallon of milk gravy. She felt that maybe some of those kids didn't have anything to eat at home. So what the hell, those "lost" chickens were giving their lives for a good cause.

At times there would be 10 or 12 horses parked outside. That is where we met when we were going to play cowboys and Indians. We would choose up sides and chase each other on horseback, all over town, until every one on one side or the other was captured and converted by tagging them. Later on we started using rubber guns. If you got shot with a good one it stung! My horse was the fastest one around and I also made a 5 shot rubber gun. That's when I got famous.

My dad had gone to work as soon as we arrived. He was working in my uncle Walter's service station. It paid a dollar a day, working from sunup to sundown. That was about $.10 an hour, the going wage for common labor, and even some skilled labor. That's all anyone was making. Of course the business men and merchants were doing a little better. He was glad to have any job. After we had been there a while, all the banks were closed by President Roosevelt. He said it was a "bank holiday" and I guess it was. Morale, at least in Little Dixie, was the lowest it had ever been. The government started giving the farmers a little money for their cattle. Then they killed them by the thousands; that helped the price a little. Those that were left were more valuable.

I later heard that after the banks closed, they received boxes and boxes of money from the government. They put it in their banks to maintain solvency, but they didn't put it in their customers accounts. Most everyone lost all the money they had in the banks. Families were devastated; wiped out completely. That period I think was when the depression bottomed out. It couldn't be much worse. That event caused many people to lose faith in the US banking system, at least the in privately owned banks. Even though the government passed a law insuring the deposits of all the people. Many people were hiding their money in jars or cans buried in their yards somewhere in the barn. For years they refused to put their money in banks.

In Europe the depression was just as bad as here, if not worse. It wasn't long before we started hearing about the "brown shirts" (nazi sympathizers) who were marching in the 4 big eastern American cities to protest the bad economic and political conditions. That was the first time anyone had ever heard of the nazi's.

* * * * * *

Sometimes during the summer, when school was out, I went with granddad on his oil and gasoline deliveries. It's true he stopped at nearly every creek to see if "they" were biting. He ranged all over that country for 50 years. Every person knew and liked him. He was a friend to all of them.

He told me a story one time from long, long ago and I have never repeated it to anyone before. Even now, i'm a little reluctant to tell it, but he has been deceased for years. He didn't make any effort to conceal it and I think it's part of the life in Little Dixie that molded the culture of the country.

A long time ago he had bought a brand new 30-30 lever action rifle. A perfectly good deer rifle for the brushy forest country in the Quachita mountains. He carried it in his truck just in case a wild turkey or deer ran out into the road and blocked his way.

When he first started delivering gasoline and oil years ago, he had finished his deliveries and had stopped to take a walk through a spot where he had seen some "signs" [deer tracks]. He knew a family of Indians that lived in the area, so he hunted around through their place and stopped for a short visit. He spent a while, had a little nip of firewater with the old man, and spent about an hour chatting about the good old days.

There was a stranger there and granddad said he kept looking at grandfathers new rifle. He would pick it up, look it over, then he would sight something, then look it over again.

This excess interest finally attracted granddads curiosity and concern, so he decided that maybe he should leave. So he thanked the family members and took up his new rifle and started walking off down the path back to his truck.

Grandfather said that as he left, the stranger also picked up his rifle and followed him down the path. So granddad walked a little faster, so did the stranger. Granddad then picked up more speed and started keeping a closer eye on the guy. Finally granddad doubled back and got behind the stranger, sure enough the stranger was stalking him, presumably he wanted to kill him and take his new rifle. After a little more tracking him, grandfather called at him, and instantly, the stranger whirled around in the firing position and grandfather killed him, with that new rifle.

That incident, although brutal and unwanted, does give you some idea of what the reality was in the early days, just before and after statehood in Oklahoma . Life had to be played out to meet the circumstances of the moment, and often someone had to take a fall.

Every saturday, in down town Valliant, was the time to shop, buy your supplies, and have it out with your enemies. I always made it a point to be in town on Saturday. You could see all the action by both big and little people that kept society going. The big boys would “urge” the younger boys from the country to fight with the younger boys from the “city” (Valliant had the city boys). They would tell each kid that the other kid had told everyone that you had “slumbered in your bed last night”. Of course that had to be bad, imagine slumbering in your bed!

Then they would tell each of them that the other had called him a lair. That was even worse! It wasn’t long until both of the kids were wound up to settle the issue. The big boys would then draw a line in the dirt, and make the kids face off each other. Then they would tell one of the kids, "did you see that? He spit on your ancestor". The kid would look down around on his britches legs. "are you going to let him get away with that"? Generally that was enough to get them fighting. That's the way it was, so help me.

There was one little guy that lived out in the country. He was as mean and aggressive as a cobra snake. He was about ten years old and wasn't very big, but he was wound up tight and would fight anyone in town. He was always spitting through a gap in his front teeth. And he could cuss like a sailor. The big guys would use him to keep a level playing field if a city boy got too big for his britches, as they would say.

The big guys would fight also. I watched a grown man chase another grown man right through the center of town with a tire iron. He finally caught up with him just as he ducked into a car. The guy brought that tire iron down to crush his skull, but instead he hit the top of the door jam on the car and bent the top in about 6 inches. He tried to kill that guy. No one did anything to stop the fight or end the chase. I think they both finally spent their energy and anger and the whole thing came to a bloodless end.

As a kid, you had to be alert to unusual sounds and actions that were taking place in town , or you would miss all the good stuff going on down there, like shootings and fights. One day I heard some gunfire. I hit the trail immediately to downtown, which was about 3 or 4 blocks. By the time I made it, the shooting was over and the results were laying on the ground in front of the bank. Some dumb, maybe drunk guys, decided to rob the Valliant bank.

They went in with guns drawn, took the money and started backing out, like in the movies. Well, When they got a few steps outside, a barrage of gunfire hit them. Nearly every man in town was armed. The grocers, service station operators, the druggist all joined in the fight. They all opened up on those two poor fellows. Of course they went down immediately. That was about the time most of us kids arrived. We missed the shooting, but we saw the futility of trying to rob a bank in Valliant. So we learned our lesson, and I'm sure the robbers learned theirs. There's a lot to say for realistic learning experiences.

Bootlegging was a good paying job. There were plenty of guys who tried it. But our old time western frontier sheriff, by the name of "Mr.(old man) Richards" made you pay a high price for your learning years. He was very hard on bootleggers, especially if they tried to get a load past him in full view of his public. He was one scary guy to us kids. He ruled our lives with an iron hand. Valliant had recently built a solid poured concrete, iron reinforced, jail house a half block off main street. If you heard or saw something strange going on, that's where you headed. Because that's where Sheriff Richard would show up with his prisoner, dead or alive.

Our sheriff had a great big handle bar mustache. He wore a big black hat. He was severely hair-lipped and tongue tied. You could not understand a single word he said. Even when he said "good morning young fellow", in the most friendly terms, it scared you to death. He wore a magnum .45 cal. Pistol, it was huge. Worse of all he limped badly. Back in his early days of law enforcement, he had pulled his gun on some one. The gun went off before he got it out of the holster, and he shot himself in the leg. That incident was never, never, never mentioned in public.

To be successful at wholesale bootlegging you had to have a fast car. The little 1935 or 36 ford v-8, I think that was the year they first used the V-8 engine, was the car to have. It was fast like a running horse. There were two brothers in our area that went into the business. They guaranteed safe delivery and on time. They had a brand new ford V-8 roadster. They would load it down until it almost dragged the rear end on the ground. They had to come through Valliant to get to Idabel, the big town in the county that was their biggest "point of sales".

When they were ''making a delivery'', you could hear them coming down the highway, long before they entered the city limits. That little V-8 was making time and screaming out loud. Sheriff Richard would hurry outside and stand on the edge of the highway and watch up the road. When they came into sight, he could see whether or not they had a load. If their rear end was real low, he would draw that "hog leg" 6 shooter and get set. When they came through town about 60 miles an hour, he would start shooting at them. He never did shoot them down in "flames", but he put a lot of holes through that little V-8 ford. After a day or two, you could go down to the body shop garage and count how many times he had hit them.

* * * * * *

Discipline was an important element of our bringing up in Little Dixie. My father took care of things when they were violations of the big important things like honesty , truthfulness, arrogance, and those kindred violations that were truly detrimental to a family's well being. Mother enforced the rules that you had to obey if you wanted to "keep living". Those were the everyday transgressions related to doing your chores, being mean to the younger children, not doing as she told us. These rules mostly related to our attitude, demeanor and responsiveness to direct orders. A pretty workable division of command and control for my parents.

This arrangement fit very well into their personalities. My mother was high strung, hot tempered and very athletic. She could outrun anyone of us. She could throw a base ball as far and as hard as anyone of us; furthermore she could hit you with it most of the time. She was a living, breathing, threat to a kid who wanted to misbehave. It wasn't beyond her to give the wrong kid a few whacks once in a while instead of the guilty one who actually caused the trouble. Then she would say, "you keep track of it and the next time you need a spanking, I will give you a free pass".

Since I was the oldest and in a position to work with her most, it seemed to me that I got into trouble a lot of the time when I was as innocent as the driven snow. But she always made it up ok. I broke about even.

When she had to, she could yank a big kid up, read the riot act to him, glare at him right in the face, rough him up, then set him down. His shirt tail would be pushed up under his arms pits in big lumps. Every button was torn off his shirt.(they were never replaced), she often jerked the nail out of his pants belt loops and the pants would fall down. And he had never been touched with hand or switch. Then sometime maybe he had been. But which ever, he didn't know what had happened to him. But he immediately reaffirmed his obedience to her rules to "keep alive by".

The word must have gotten out in the family that if you could run around and around her when she was trying to give you an unannounced spanking, it didn't hurt so much. I tried it one time. I had made a couple of loops with her holding on to my hand, when all of a sudden she took a step backward and kept her hand out away from her body far enough so that the next turn around I had to come in front of her; that put me right the center of her heaviest fire power. I never tried that again .

My dad was different. He took care of the big important violations, like treason, lying to him, not keeping your word or the family honor. He did it differently, he would say, "i want to talk to you guys in a couple of hours. So come back to me then". That was our survival evaluation period. Should I go off and join the French Foreign Legion or should I be there when he asked me to?

Generally when we had a problem that dad was to settle, two or three of the boys had messed up and/or denied knowing anything about anything. Perhaps some one had reported us for something we had done. It seems that he always knew ahead of time exactly what we had done; like denting the car door and it wouldn't close shut. Some little, minor, unimportant thing like that. He assured us that the door was not the subject, it was our denial!

During this 2 hour time period time we had sweated giant drops of sweat. Finally the moment of truth. He would explain what he expected from his kids, especially me, I was the oldest and I or we had not met those standards. So, what did we think the punishment should be? On and on, we discussed the factors involved. The pros and cons. What should he do to impress on us the importance of truthfulness and good behavior.? Did we know that our actions were not acceptable? We were getting too old now to spank, but if this type of behavior occurred again, he may have to do that very thing to make a lasting impression. After he had scared us to the point of death, we were praying that it was a "go and sin no more" type of punishment. Most of the time it was , and it was very effective! He rarely physically punished us boys and never in my life did I see him ever punish one of the girl children. He was one fine dad.

We did have the ordinary social and family problems in Little Dixie. I suppose the present day sociologist would attribute it to poverty and lack of opportunity. If that were a major contributor, nearly everyone at that time would have been in jail. We didn't have any more misfits and some will say that we had fewer social problems then, than we do now, and just look at the difference in the national average income in the two periods.

Some Dr.Yahoo is on the public radio right now saying that too many poor people in one place makes everyone deteriorate even poorer and they will take to drugs and crime. So the government should spend millions to move poor folks (like we were) into a well to do neighborhood. God! I sure hope that will solve the problem of poverty.

Our western frontier Sheriff Richards had the same kind of problems.once in a while. There was this family in town. They were really poor, they had family troubles, and I admit they caused the Sheriff a lot of problems. For instance, one of the family members had a drinking problem. She was a very beautiful young girl and it was hard to imagine her being violent about anything. She looked like an angel. But when she nipped a little too much she became mean and would attack and beat the devil out of the other members of her family. They would go down town and get the sheriff to come out and take the wild one down to the new concrete jail they had built.

When the sheriff came out to their house, she would start kicking and screaming at the top of her voice. It was a hard job even for him to get her put in the jail. That was what a bunch of kids looked forward to, When we heard the hollering and the cussing, we would run down town to the jail and watch the violent show of making her go into the jailhouse. We did learn a lot of new cuss words. This one time we made it down there just as he finally got her in the jail and the door to her cell closed and locked.

There was a little hallway between the two cells inside, like a dogtrot hallway. The sheriff, Old Man Richards had just about all the interference from his audience he could put up with by this time, so he asked us kids if we would like to go in and see her. Oh yes! That would be fun. So we went into the dogtrot, and then, he slammed the big outside iron door shut. We were closed in. We hadn't planned on that! The wild one really put on a violent show. She slung her jail furniture around off the walls, cussed like a drunken sailor, and tried to grab us through the bars, she spit on us and generally scared the hell out of everyone. In a few minutes, the sheriff opened the big outside door and told us kids to get out of there and go home. He was having enough problems with the wild one, so scoot. We never did get trapped inside again, never ever again.

On one end of the jailhouse was a little window just about kid high. It had iron bars on it but no glass window or screens. So it was a perfect place to peek in and see what the wild one or anyone else was doing while in jail. The next day, some of the kids thought it would be fun to peek in while the wild one was there. They did, she was very nice to them for a little while. But not for long. Now I didn't see this or was I involved in this event. But I was told by someone in the group that did participitated in the event. The wild one, suddenly pick up her "night jar" and dumped it through the window, right in their faces. Sooo, stay away from the jail window when the wild one is in residence!

I guess the Dr. Yahoo on the radio is right, too much poverty in a close area does lead to crime. During the next day or two, the wild one had set fire to the mattress and everything else they had inside the jail. I think sheriff richards figured he better let her out, she was tearing up his jail. See, dr yahoo is correct. Living in poverty and close quarters does create crime and violence.

* * * * * *

When school was out in the summer time, we took to the river for swimming and fishing. "little river" was only about 3 or 4 miles from town. That's where we spent the summer. We could walk or hitch a ride if we were lucky. We knew where every watermelon field was on the way. Where the peanut shocks were, where ever fruit orchard and wild plum thicket was in the country . We could leave right after breakfast and get to the river in a couple of hours. We would swim all day, then we would scrounge every orchard for fruit, ripe or green, or we would steal a watermelons or two on the way back to town. We would stop at the place where the muscadines were and eat a pocketful on the way home. We would then angle over and get a pocketful of peanuts drying in big shocks. When we got home we were still starved to death. Mother always had a great big supper fixed for us. Those were the good old days. I don't think poverty and limited advantages stunted our growth very much and it certainly did not stunt our joy in living.

Even though I didn't have any more fights for a while, I felt that there was an undertone of hostility from the 2 or 3 leading kids in the town. Their fathers were the big merchants there. They had saddles, cowboy boots to wear and really all the things a growing boy would want. They lifted weights, exercised their muscles, with all sorts of gadgets. They went to little social events that most of the other guys did not attend. I didn't care about their social life, but I didn't want to get cross ways with them either. From time to time I would get a message that someone in the group was going to "take me on".

But it never did go further than that- just talk. Finally the rumors came to a head. The main jock in town sent me a note. Now this jock was, most of the time, a really good friend of mine. We rode together and played ball on the same team. I couldn't understand why he thought I was a threat to his position. I didn't give a damn about being head man in their gang. But the fear was in him. I think his grunts felt that I was a threat to them, and they were pushing the jock to put an end to my threat. They were afraid to do it. So, they were forcing him to do it.

The arrangements were made. One day we would meet after church and have it out. The whole thing was unusual. I hadn't been to church twice all the time I had lived there. But I didn't care where the battle field was I would be there. I told my mother about the event. She was a little concerned that I might get hurt if they ganged up on me. So we talked it over and developed a plan that would make the fight a little more equal. My opponent was much heavier than I was. He had been building up his muscles by weight lifting. It wasn't going to be a very equal match. I finally figured why he wanted to do it after church. All his support flunkies would be there to see it and could verify the victory and they could help him if he needed it. Earlier, he had even bought a punching bag and was training on it. Things did not look very encouraging for me. I told my mother that I probably couldn't beat him in a fair fight. So she made a suggestion.

She would help me get ready. So we took a rope about 6 feet long, doubled it, tied the two ends together in a big hard knot, and soaked it in water all afternoon until about an hour before church. We took it out of the water and dried it off as well as we could. I stuffed it down my britches leg with the knot on the bottom end. Then I went to church by myself. I really didn't want to fight the jock. We were getting along with each very well. But his stooges would not let things stay as they were.

During church the he kept looking over at me with a silly grin on his face. I know he did not expect to see me there that night. I would look at him and nod my head just a little, "like buster you are a dead man". Finally church let us sinners out. I walked outside and stopped on the sidewalk right on the front walk. I turned around and waited until he came out with his stooges. He walked up and I said , "I don't have any reason to fight you except that you asked me to do it". "ok", I told him. "I'm ready, but first let me tell you what I am going to do to you. I have a weapon in my britches leg. One end is as hard as a rock and about as big as your fist. The instant you come toward me i'm going to knock your head off with it. I might even kill you, but i'm not going to let you beat up on me. Further more, I'm not going to run from you". Then, "hey, look", he said , "if you are not going to fight fair, I'm not going to fight any other way". Then I told him again, "I'm not going to fight you fair, I don't think I can whip you, but I'm damn sure not afraid to try". He answered me that "well, "I'm not going to fight you if that's the way it is". So he turned around and walked off. That was one time I was glad not to have to go all the way. He was not a coward. He and I both were glad we had found a way to end it without violence.

* * * * * *

Poverty was still hanging heavy over Little Dixie with a tenacious grip. A little later as times got even worse, dad told me we had to sell “old Ben”. That was a real blow to me. From that moment on, I truly believe that Ben knew that we had to end our long friendship. I could hardly stand to even think about not having him. We both knew we wouild never be together again. I think dad got $5.00 for him. He bought groceries for us kids with the money.

Ben and I really understood each other. I could tell he had a soul, just like I did. Yes, I hugged and held old Ben in my arms and cried uncontrollably when they took him away.

I guess it’s ok to tell a little sentimental horse story once in a while. You would be surprised how many people do believe that their favorite pet is more than just an animal without a holy spirit of some sort. I think the theologians are wrong on that little point. Ben had a soul, if I had one. The theologians aren’t perfect in all aspects.

Valliant was the shopping center of the area. It had one bank, two service stations, two garages, two drug stores, 3 or 4 little grocery stores, 2 hardware stores, and one cafe. It’s industrial base was a cotton gin, a saw mill and a place to sell hand made arts and crafts, like railroad ties. Oh yes, it had a half dozen bootleggers and a concrete steel reinforced jail. Everyone else was trying to farm to make a living.

The farmers were the lucky ones. They ate as well then as we eat today and they lived a more active life. They exercised strenuously every day. They went hiking a lot, from one end of the cotton patch to the other, row on row. Those were the good old healthy, wholesome days. They got lots of sunshine and they had healthy odoriferous air to breath, from the exhaust of natures power plants, a robust pair of mules that had eaten only natural products.

* * * * * *

Valliant had a modern airport, for it's day. Eighty acres of smooth open prairie pasture, a 1000 yards from down town. While I lived there we had an airplane land one day. My god! I ran faster than I ever had before to watch it land and maybe I could touch it and see the pilot. I felt that some great person was surely flying that airplane. When I got there he was a great person.

An army air corps pilot got out of the plane. And he was standing there in all the glory of the "coming of the lord". His leather jacket flung open and his white silk scarf hanging down to the tops of his leather officers boots. I stood there in awe of the power of the almighty. When he got organized, he began to help his female passenger out of the single cockpit they had both been riding in. The airplane was a two wing, single seated, army air corp fighter plane. He was bringing his favorite bunkey back home after a wild weekend they had somewhere near the Lawton, Oklahoma Fort sill army camp. At least that was my take on it!

The pilot arranged for one of the on-lookers to take his girl friend to her home, and then come back by the service station and bring him 5 gallons of water for his radiator. His engine had been running a little hot. He wanted to top off his radiator tank to be sure he could make it back to his base. While the guys were gone, I stood around and listened to the older fellows talk to him. I stood close to the airplane and actually touched it. It didn't take but about 30 minutes for the water to arrive. The pilot stood up on one of his wheels, took the cap off the radiator, and poured the water into the tank.

He thanked the guys that had helped him. He put on all his flying clothes, put on his parachute and goggles. He saluted his admirers and got in the cockpit. He motioned everyone to move back out of the way, and then he started cranking her up. It fired for a couple of seconds, then stopped dead. He cranked her again, same thing. He tried again, not one pop. She was dead as a doornail. It never did kick over again. There were a dozen kids and men watching this whole thing.

Finally, he stood up on his seat, slung his leg out of the cockpit and stood on the ground, embarrassed and dumbfounded. After a few suggestions from everyone in the crowd he was still dumbfounded. It had been ok less than a hour before. It had been running perfectly. He walked around his engine trying to find something wrong, got upon his wheel again , and again he couldn't find anything wrong anywhere.

Then all of a sudden he had a flash of genius. He said "I poured that damn water in my gas tank". Every one agreed that he had really messed up. But, he was smart enough to wait 15 or 20 minutes to let the water settle to the bottom of his fuel tank, then he could open the drain valve and let the water flow out. That's what he did. Then he tried again and it ran like a sweet angel.

We all waved goodbye, and off he flew into the sunset back toward Fort Sill. I bet he was having second thoughts about whether the fun he had on the weekend was really worth all the trouble and embarrassment he had. Maybe not, but then, maybe yes.

My interest in aviation doubled every time I had an encounter with an airplane or any one involved with aircraft. I was the "paper boy" for the "Paris morning news". I had a paper route in Valliant with 15 to 20 customers. The weekly charge was $.10 cents, the news paper company in Paris got $.05 and I got $.05 cents a week for each customer. If I sold an extra for $.05, I could keep that. About 20% of the customers never paid on time. Then half of those never did pay me. So if I cleared $.75 cents a week for the whole job, that wasn't bad!

One day the headline in the paris news was the "death of Will Rogers and Wiley post" at Point Barrow , alaska. Wiley Post was a famous flyer in the early days. He had just set a world record altitude for pressurized flight. He had used a modified divers helmet and suit to fly to the record altitude. He was one of my heroes. I sold about 12 "extras" that day. Of course Will Rogers was a famous Oklahoma part Indian. He lived on the northern most border of Little Dixie.

The next school year I would be in the 7th grade. That's getting on up there. By that time I was hitchhiking all around the country. Three or four of us would hitch to Wright city to see the annual rodeo. One time I hitched to Paris, Texas for a picnic given to all the paper boys that delivered the Paris news. That was a great time but I had to walk the last 8 or 10 miles back home. It got dark and there were no cars on the road.

One day my father told me there was going to be an airshow in Idabel on saturday, the next weekend. And further more he would let me have a quarter to ride the bus down there. Or, I could hitch hike down and ride the bus back. I chose to hike back. I was down there early on the morning of the show. As a matter of fact, I got there before the airplanes did. But what a show they had. Of course they were carrying passengers, at $5.00 for a 10 minute ride. But they also did stunts, off and on during the day. There was a parachute jump that was very exciting to watch. They also had a "forced landing with a dead engine" act. All this was absolutely new to me. So I stayed until all the airplanes were gone. Then I tried to hitch home. About sundown, I finally got a ride on the front fender of a empty log truck headed for the mountains north of Valliant. I nearly froze to death on that ride but it was worth it!

We didn't know what it meant to be afraid to be out at all times during the night or in strange unknown towns, trying to hitch a ride home. We roamed the towns, the woods, and the whole Indian country up in the mountains. We kids went unescorted on camping trips. We hunted and fished and swam in ever creek and river over two feet deep. We all carried guns and hunting knives and no one was ever hurt or got into trouble. I think that is a better testimony on how to raise kids than what all the scientific and social education and parental training tells us to follow today. I think many of the pundits are right, to say "what are we doing wrong?" I will hazard a guess, that we need to have more parents who have and enforce a set of rules that their children need, "to live by", rather than parent's with career paths that their children must live and compete with.

* * * * * *

Our family finances gradually got better. My father got a job surveying all the farm land in McCurtain county.and it was one of the largest counties in the state. The government had started a program of assigning acreage allotments to the farmers and telling them how much land they could put under cultivation. It was the "AAA" farm program started under president Roosevelt. My dad got the first job. The only thing wrong was, he had no way to travel over the county; so he started walking to work. He had a fairly large load to carry, such as a surveying table, sighting rod, marker sticks and a measuring tape, plus his personal things. It wasn't a back breaking load but it was clumsy to carry around. But off he went. He would be gone for most of the week; then he would come back home, rest up a day or two, then off he would go and repeat the whole thing. It surely must have been like a little trail of tears.

After a few months, he bought the pieces to an old worn-out Willis Overland pickup truck. The salesman towed the front part of the pickup to our house and parked it in our barn. About two days later, here my father came down the sidewalk carrying a replacement rear end and drive shaft over his shoulder. He had to remove the existing one; it had stripped all the teeth off the rear end gears. We were finally going to have a car. He worked on that thing about a week or two. Finally the day came to see if it would run. Since he had to crank it, he showed me what to do in the drivers seat while he cranked. That was a proud day. He had also told me that I could learn to drive it.

Well, believe it or not, that darn little thing started and ran without a hitch. At least it seemed ok to us. We had never owned a gear shift car before. Actually he had not learned how to drive a manual shift car. He had learned to drive a "t" model ford, which was mostly foot work. But what the heck, he had been told what to do, so he cranked her up. He didn't know how things worked so, I had to get out for the test drive. Off down the alley he went. After a while, here he came back from the other direction. It still was all in one piece. He wasn't sure how to stop. But as he came up to the barn, he just cut off the switch and it humped and jumped to a complete stop.

He drove it to work for two or three days. He got more confidence and then it was my time. He explained about the shifting and clutch work. He explained how you coordinated the gas and the release of the clutch. After ten or fifteen minutes of intense training, we headed out for sawmill road. It was getting dark and there would be no traffic out that late. This pickup had no top over the cab. It didn't even have any doors or backs for the seats. You just sat on a flat board Bench someone had built behind the steering wheel. We hadn't tried the lights to see if they would work. So away we go, him telling me every step of the way how to drive the car; most of it for the first time for both of us.

The sawmill was a mile or so away. By the time we got there, we had to turn on the lights. They were so inadequate that you could not tell if they were on or not. So, we stopped for a moment and dad got out to take a look. We had one, and fortunately it was on the drivers side. That was adequate.

This little old country road had a set of permanent wagon wheel impression in it. They were hardened almost into rock. Well, I got down into those darn things and I couldn't get my wheels out to save my life. I know that we were not going 5 miles an hour, and it was a good thing. The car tracks were a little different in width from the wagon tracks. If I got one wheel out, then the two or three others would jump either in or out. That jerked the car violently from one side to the other. Back and forth we went. Finally dad had me stop and he took over. In a few feet he was doing the same thing. My, he can be cranky some times. We finally got to a cross road and he turned us around and we went home. He said that I would get another lesson tomorrow or maybe the next day. I could hardly wait.

After a couple more trial runs, he said I was ready to solo. When the day came, I headed for saw mill road. There was no traffic to contend with, but those darn wagon tracks were still there, I had managed to learn how to stay out of them. So down across the TO&E railroad tracks [that was a little private railroad that hauled timber out of the mountains], then on past the sawmill. I was doing great. That was the slow part, when I got to the smooth graveled crossroads I stepped on the gas a little and I bet I went 20 miles an hour. It was so thrilling, I stood up so that my head was sticking above the windshield. I had a mile of straight open road ahead. Gosh, I was living high on the hog!

We kept that little Willis Overland a short time. Then dad had a chance to trade it for a ford "t'' model pickup. He was more familiar with the Ford, and I guess the little Willis was falling apart again.

The ford "t" model was more difficult for me. It had no shift and the starting procedure was more complex. It had a magneto and you had to work the ignition differently. Be that as it may, whenever we went to the river, I could get it started if the boys would push me. There were always a half dozens boys that wanted to go along. So, they would push, and when I got it running, I would go really slow as long as I could. They would run alongside and jump on if they could, if not they stayed home. When we got to the river there was a little hill I would park on. When we finished the day, they could all get aboard, then one or two would shove us off the hill and I could get it started by coasting down the hill. The whole operation worked as smooth as silk.

Dad was doing better. Having a car certainly helped his attitude. He got a raise or two. He also got a little more budget to hire a helper. Surveying is really a two man job. In the very beginning he had to get the farmers to help him; and quite often they would house and feed him when he was surveying their farms. For a while he paid me $. 50 a day to be his stick man. When school started, I lost my job. The depression still had a hold on Little Dixie!

The last little brother, born shortly after we had moved to Valliant was number 7, that was it! That is all! 5 boys and 2 girls, fini! My parents always insisted that we get an education, maybe even a college degree. But at that time in our life the big problem was to keep all 7 of us alive and well fed.

* * * * * *

Just behind our house, there lived a wonderful black woman, named "Besse". She had no family that we knew of. She was always alone, except for our bunch of kids. When we moved in we didn't know anything about her. She was just always there. I suppose she was a perfect example of the hopeless and abandoned blacks that existed all over the country at that time. She "mothered" all of us kids. We were welcome to come to her house anytime we wanted something to eat or needed something done like getting a hole patched or anything fixed we had broken. Besse would take care of it.

Jerry, our next to the youngest decided that Besse was his. She accepted the responsibility and they became fast friends. Anything baby Jerry wanted , Jerry got. He would always eat one meal of some kind with her every day. She would cook what baby Jerry wanted. Boy, and you did not mistreat baby Jerry when Besse was around. She would be on your case immediately. We considered Besse as our second mother. This relationship went on until much later when we had to move away. The goodbye between her and baby Jerry was heart breaking. It was almost wordless, a quite personel expression of childlike love. Besse was torn between staying in Valliant and asking if she could move with us and continue to live with our family. There can be heart breaking drama, even when unspoken, between the very lonely and the very innocent. Yes, even in Little Dixie.

Gradually all the kids started growing up and taking on their own personality. Mother was always amazed, no two of her kids were any thing alike. Everyone liked to eat different things. Each wanted his own place at the table, and you had better not fudge over the boundary. Each one had his favorite piece of fried chicken. There would be a real ruckus if you got the wrong one. The continual struggle for each of our rights was no doubt tiring to mother. Every once in a while she would clean the whole bunch out of the house. Or she would resolve any questions on the spot. At least that would quiet things down for a while. You may not agree with her decision, but for the time being that's the way it was.

I tried to give away or trade off the milking chore a hundred times, but I could never make a deal, with anyone. Occasionally I would get so disgusted with the job, that I would rebel as far as I could, without going over the limits of the rules that I could live by. One sunday morning I had just about had all of that damn job I could stand. I pushed it to the limit. I stalled and complained and complained and stalled some more. Finally about 9 o'clock in the morning, which is very late so far as the cows were concerned, I was still being hard to get along with. My mother called me into the kitchen, she said wanted to "give me something".

Hey! I might be making some headway on getting rid of this milking job. When I walked into the kitchen she was standing there with this two gallon Mrs.Tuckers lard bucket in her hand. I walked up to her, fully expecting to negotiate the new milking chores. Well, she drew that bucket back and whacked me over the head with it. It bent almost double, completely down to my ears on each side! I saw a bright flash of light before my eyes.

It wasn't all from the bucket blow, it was mostly from the surprise lesson I just had in child psychology. She handed me the bucket and said "now you straighten that milk bucket out and go milk those cows like I told you". I replied with a smart, "O. K". The impact did not really hurt me, but it convinced me that I was not a very good negotiator.

Our uncle Walter Ross was grandmothers brother. He was a funny old fellow. He had spent most of his life working in the coal mines in Alabama some where around Birmingham, I believe. He owned the biggest gas station in Valliant. Even during the deepest part of the depression, uncle Walt had some money. No one knew how much or where he made it; probably in the coal mines. If he took in 10 cents a day, he saved 5 of it. He was as tight as bark on a tree in business matters. But generally he gave us kids a piece of candy if we were hanging around the station. He probably wanted us to go home, but he was always good to us.

One day, right out of the blue, he decided he wanted to go to Alaska. He had never been up north and that sounded like fun. He sold his station to one of his workers for little or nothing, bought a new ford coupe, loaded all his personal stuff in it and headed for Seattle Washington. He planned to take the steamboat up the coastal waterway to Alaska. No one heard squat from him for a few weeks. We all thought he never will make it. He will stop along the way and buy another gas station and settle down. Most of us thought he had lost his mind. Everything had been so impulsive.

But he was too old to learn a new lesson this late. In about four or five weeks here he came back into town and resettled in another gas station in Valliant. The family was afraid to ask what had happened. But one day he was talking to granddad and he volunteered an answer. He told grandaddy that he had taken a cabin on a freighter and had gone all the way to alaska. They had docked at some city, I think it was in Anchorage, just at dark one afternoon, too late to get off and hunt a room. So he stayed in his cabin overnight. He woke up next morning, went out on the deck to see what Alaska looked like. He didn't like the way it looked, so he booked his same cabin back to the good old U S of A. He stayed on the ship all time they were unloading and reloading. He never did go ashore or set foot on the Alaskan ground. He had decided that he wanted to come back home. I'm sure all that didn't seem strange to him.

President Roosevelt's new anti poverty programs had been passed and were having a large effect on the nation's way of doing business. The whole alphabet soup of national legislation such as CCC, WPA, AAA and a host of other changes were doing some good in Little Dixie. Especially those programs that gave immediate relief to farmers. They did get the economy awake after years of stagnation. Up north most of the factories had closed. Those that were still open were tangled up in labor wars.

But, the greatest of all the changes on the horizon were the conflicts that were coming from Europe. Hitler was making trouble in Europe. Spain's Franco had started a war in Spain. Mussolini had attacked Ethiopia. The awful prospect of war was every where. America at that time had a very solid bunch of isolationists in congress. No one was going to let America get into the wars that were going on in the rest of the world. The vast atlantic ocean was our security blanket. We were safe from all foreign wars. Oh, yeah!

* * * * * *

In 1936 everything in our family was getting better. We had moved to Idabel Okla. Dad had a big promotion in the new AAA farm program. Even I , the worlds greatest cow milker, had gotten a good paying job. I was sweeping out the county's AAA farm program office building in Idabel. Purely a case of blatant nepotism. I was making $2.00 a month. I swept it out, emptied the waste baskets and gave it a general dusting every day. I was a federal employee. Although I was a government employee, I still had to milk our cows. I will be saddled with that job for the next 4 years, if I had known that, I probably would have .... That was my problem then, what the hell could I have done? Oh this cruel and brutal world!

When we moved to Idabel, dad had received a really big raise. He was now earning $90.00 a month. That was big time! We moved into a nice home, still without inside facilities, but very nice. Now maybe I could go to school without getting into a useless fight with some nut who thought he was invincible. I was in the 9th grade that year. They called us freshmen. During the first class of the first day our teacher was gone for a while. We were filling out some kind of paper work for chemistry class. At least we were in the chemical laboratory with the big tables and such. Eventually some one started shooting paper wads with rubber bands, those wet soggy kind that splatter.

The local boys were having such a good time hitting the little girls with paper wads and making them yell. I thought, I bet I can do that! So I chewed up a nice large wet, soggy, loose one, let it go toward a girl across the room. It splattered right in the center of her forehead. She saw me shoot it. I had no defense. Well, she came up over that table after me. She actually crossed over the row of tables , yelling violent epitaphs at me and I was as guilty as sin. The only thing I could do was run, [yes our rules said it was ok to run from girls] and I did. For months I had to look out for that gal. She was my nemesis for a whole semester.

Idabel was a big town as far as I was concerned. It had two theaters, with 2 picture shows going at the same time. That was the most important form of entertainment for us. We learned very quickly that the saturday show was the thing. They had a cowboy show with Tom Mix or Hoot Gibson or Tim McCoy and a weekly serial, generally about tarzan or flash gordon, [he was our very first astronaut], Dale, his main squeeze and Dr. Zarkov, the evil ruler of some unknown planet. Flash, was never harmed, Dale was never kissed, and Dr. Zarkov was never caught. The cowboy show and the serial repeated over and over all day saturday. I know it cycled at least 7 times in one day because I have watched the same show repeat that many times on saturday.

The conditions in Europe became the central political problem for us. Lindbergh and other isolationist were downplaying the Germans intent. Our representatives in congress were crying peace!, Peace! But the talk of war did not stop. The few who wanted to prepare for war were shouted down. Congress did nothing. We were safe they said. Congress even refused to loan the British a bunch of old rusty destroyers from WW1, we had put in mothballs, up in a northern port.

In spite of all the war clouds, life went on in Little Dixie. Jean and I were playing in the band at high school. She was getting really good. She played the oboe. I guess that is one of the most difficult instruments there is to play. I was playing the big bb flat bass. It's one of the heaviest and bulkiest. John had grown up tall, so he was playing basket ball. Reynolds was still in middle school. The rest of the kids were strung out in the middle and elementary schools.

When we enrolled in the new schools we had to have a new rule added to our "rules we lived by." Being the oldest, I was made responsible to even the score if any big kids jumped on our little brothers and sisters. That increased the scope of my responsibility. But, as long as the kids were the same size, within reason, I was to do nothing. But for a gross mismatch, it was my job to "make him pay", and forever more desist. We had not encountered this problem while we lived in the country or a small community type town. But in Idabel, it had become a problem.

I didn't care, I was expedienced at mixing it up when necessary. I didn't look for it but I didn't hide either, It finally came to pass. Some big old slew footed overgrown bully roughed up one of the kids. Maybe he was messing with both John and Reynolds I don't remember the details. We decided to let it go, for a little while. If it didn't happen again we would forget it.

Some time later, Reynolds came home crying. This big goose had been pushing and shoving him down. Reynolds was much smaller than John and John was much smaller than the bully. That put him in my class. Ok, I'll find him and clean his plow. I had seen this guy before. He was a typical overgrown Neanderthal bully type guy.

On my paper route one day, I saw him playing with some other kids down the road a bit; so I turned off my regular route and went down by his house.

He saw me coming and I saw him go up to his front door then come back out in the yard. When I got down to his house I walked up to him and told him, "I'm going to whip your a—". He asked why was that? I told him that "you whipped my little brother, and I am going to even the score". He denied even knowing who Reynolds was. But I knew he was lying. So I popped him one. At that instant, his mother came running out of the house, screaming and yelling like a mad woman. She ran up behind me and grabbed my arms and held me tight. She started yelling at him, "hit him son", "son, hit him", "kill him, kill him son".

Well her son could not see very well right then. I had just poked a fist in his eye. But I was in a fix. If that yahoo ever did hit me it would have hurt. I started stomping her feet behind me and jabbing my elbows in her stomach. I broke loose and she went back upon her porch and called her big stupe of a kid to come in the house. She said I'm going to call the police ! I just turned and walked off. I never did hear from the police.

The second chapter to this fracas came about a year or so later, one night after a football game. I should have known that Neanderthal was not going to forget that episode.

I was bringing my big bass horn back to the band hall after the game. I had taken a little short cut footpath along the dark side of the school house, when all of a sudden this same guy stepped out from behind one of the buildings along the road, and said, "hey you, just a minute". I stopped and said, "what do you want"? He said, "do you remember last year when you jumped on me". I told him I did, but it was because he had beaten up my little brother. "I'm going to whip you now", he said. I noticed a little movement in the shadows near by, then another one. There were two or three other guys hidden in the shadows next to the building. Boy, that put a different light on the situation.

I asked him if he would wait until I put up my horn in the band hall, which wasn't 50 yards away. I told him I would be right back and we would settle the score. He said "no you won't come back. "yes I will, I promised yes I will, cross my heart". "Ok" he said "now you better come back". "Ok I will", then I left.

I went in the band hall and hung the horn in its place. The band master came in. I was hunting an iron stove poker that I had seen there before. He asked me, "what the heck are you looking for"? I told him the whole story and he said, "you just stay in here and I will call the police and they will stop this thing". I told him, no, that I was going to be ok. I had found the poker by then and was looking for a leather strap I had seen around. I found that and tied the strap to the poker and then around my wrist. The idea was that they couldn't take the poker away from me and hit me with it. I knew I was in for a gang attack. That was obvious. But I told the bandmaster again that I was ok and I could handle the situation. Then I went outside to the very spot I had stood in before.

I said, "now you bastard, I know you've got a couple of guys back there in the shadows. If you or any one of them back there in the dark make a move toward me I'm going to crush your head with this poker." And I brought it up so he could see it. "Besides I'm going to knock their heads off if they come near me. Now I have this thing tied to my arm and you cannot hit me with it, even if you can get a hold of it. So now if you are ready, come on and get me. But when you do, you are going to be the first one that gets his brains knocked out". I brought the poker up about like you would a baseball bat you were getting ready to swing.

Silence, all silence, not one peep out of any one. I told him that I had no hard feelings toward him, but he wasn't going to kick my little brothers around any more, and I better never hear of that again. "Oh", he said, "I didn't mean anything, I was just playing with them". That ended that.

I'm sure there is plenty of "scientific evidence" that shows how environment influences the development of a child. Also, how it effects the kind of citizen he turns out to be. Many good and fine children are raised in all sorts of circumstances of poverty and disadvantages. Some will be good, some will turn out bad. Certainly the negative circumstances brought on by the great depression could have been worse. But not very much worse and have the nation survive. Those of us who lived in the country and outlying regions had plenty to eat and a very healthy way of life. But, we had no money, or any of the city advantages of museums, concerts, and artistic or cultural endeavors to enjoy. I still don't know whether or not that makes one bit of difference in the final product.

Every kid I knew had access to several guns of all kinds. There were bootleggers on every corner. There were a few good ole boy's card and domino gambling dens. I didn't know a single kid or any grownups that were into dope. Yet, we had loco weed (that's the old name for marijuana) growing wild every where. We swiped and ate watermelons and peaches and peanuts, depending on what was in season. We really didn't consider that sort of thing a crime. After we had eaten the watermelons, in an hour or so, we were up in the owners yard playing with his kids. His kids had probably helped us swipe them.

It may be that we are using the natural, and for the most part the harmless, misbehaving of children, as the evidence of a crime wave. When in reality it is parental child neglect, particularly the lack of effective set of children's rules and discipline. Did you ever get involved in an adult group activity without knowing who was in charge and what the ground rules were. Most adults would have a fit if those things were not spelled out clearly in the beginning. Why shouldn't a child be confused and frustrated when he is not sure of the ground rules and who is in charge?

* * * * * *

One time in my life I was really scared and needed my mother or dad badly. I felt sure that I was in real trouble. It was when we lived in Valliant. One day when I was downtown, out of the clear blue sky, "old man" Sheriff Richards came up to me and told me to go home and tell my mother what I did. He said something about "me stealing peaches". He scared the hell out of me. I ran home as fast as I could and she was not there. I needed one of my parents right now. I needed them to get me out of this trouble. Mother was not there and I damn near died of worry and confusion and fear. God, I wanted to tell her about Sheriff Richards threat.

The day before, my two criminal friends and I had been fishing all day and we were starved to death. Since it was quite a distance home, we decided that if we had a pocket full of green peaches from a stranger's orchard on the way back, we could make it home. So we climbed over his fence and helped ourselves. He saw us and knew us; then he must have called the sheriff "old man Richards", the scariest man alive. We ate those peaches and threw the seed down all the way to town. That was the criminal evidence that convicted us. That was the story sheriff Richards told me that afternoon, when I saw him down at the service station.

He showed me an old piece of paper and he said it was an arrest warrant. He told me to go home and tell my mother exactly what I had done and get her to pack me some extra clothes and for me to come back down town. Because, he was going to put me in that damn concrete jail, and no telling how long I would be there. I could barely understand just a few words that monster told me. So I took off like a bullet. That's when I needed my parents. I was in deep doo doo and I didn't know what to do.

When I got home she wasn't there, she had gone somewhere for a few hours. I didn't know where. I packed a pair of overalls and a little shirt in a pillow case and waited. I had decided I was going to runaway to the mountains and never come back. I carried those things around for an hour. I couldn't leave and I couldn't take a chance that the sheriff would come and get me. I sure wished that I could talk to my mom or dad and explain my problems. But no, she was out and gone somewhere. That was a long and lonely afternoon.

I wonder how other kids feel whose mother and dad are never there during the day, so they can handle their little life shattering problems?

Finally she came home. I ran out and told her the whole truth and nothing but the truth. You cannot imagine how much it helped me to unload my problem onto her. It felt so good, good ,good. She immediately told me not to worry about it. She was pretty sure that old man Richards was just doing his job, and that she would go see him and he would not put me in jail. She knew that he was just scaring the hell out of us kids and that everything would be ok. "but don't do that any more", she told me. We had bushels of peaches in our own yard. We could have all we wanted. She never did talk to the sheriff.

He was the sheriff in Valliant when she was a kid. It might have been that she had a similar experience with him when she was young. That man knew how to solve the juvenile delinquency problems in the little town of Valliant. He didn't need any government program to do it.

* * * * * *

My interest and career thoughts continued to go toward airplanes. My mother's younger brother, T.C. Reynolds, was about 10 or 12 years older than I was. His interest was also fully on airplanes, and the careers that were opening up in aviation. He had enrolled in the university of Oklahoma . He was a very smart and popular boy in high school. He was real good at base ball and swimming. He was one of the few that could do a flip and a half off of the medium high diving board. That got him a lot of the attention from the little girls in high school. He was also a very good piano player. To be honest, he was a real jock.

He graduated from Valliant high school some time along in the early thirties. He went to the university of Oklahoma . He was taking engineering. In his senior year, he decided to enlist in the naval aviators flight training school in Pensacola, Florida. He graduated as a pilot and was commissioned as a Lt. JG. A year or so before the Japanese attack on pearl harbor . He was stationed in Hawaii and was flying the big PBY flying boat on submarine patrols. His success in the flight training program just set me on fire to be a navy pilot.

That was it! I had to go to college and take aeronautical engineering. I must be a pilot. Getting a degree was the mandantory advice I got from him and my father. Dad told me that flying alone was a starvation career. I must take all the heavy math and science programs I could get while I was in high school. With a college degree, I could earn a living while flying around having fun. My career path was cast in concrete.

Little Dixie really had changed by 1936 and 37. If you wanted work you could get it. The pay was pretty low but you could make a living. Logging and other common labor work was available. Farming was losing out to cattle raising. Most of the farmland was not good enough to make any money. The farmers were turning into cattlemen and their farms were turning into ranches.

Roosevelt was really trying to get the nation to become aware of the events taking place in Europe. Hitler had come from behind his pretense of protecting the German peoples "rights" in the various parts of Europe. He was invading the little countries around him. Roosevelt will shortly order 50000 airplanes for the army to begin the rebuilding of our armed forces in response to the threats from germany. The draft was inevitable.

By the late 30's there were very few orchards around. No one was shocking peanuts anymore. Heck, a kid could starve to death in this country now. Farms are being turned into pastures. The quail hunting was no good. The draft board was into operation. Little Dixie was changing right before our eyes. There was a major exodus of young men into the military. There were no industries in Little Dixie to take up the slack in the income of the families that were sending their boys to war. Young people were leaving to get good jobs in the new armaments effort. All in all Little Dixie was not getting along very well. My dad had been promoted to the top position in the AAA office in Idabel. My parents were doing ok. They were planning to build a new home.

I had a small scholarship to go to southeastern state college in Tishimingo, Oklahoma after high school if I would play in their band. My sister, Emily Jean would graduate next year then John a year later. The nest is being emptied rather quickly. Mother and Dad were going to move up town right across the street from the high school. They moved in shortly before I graduated from high school.

In the early 40s, everyone knew that the war was close, but no one wanted to do anything about it. President Roosevelt was trying his best to get the nation fired up enough to demand some action, if not down right intervention. He finally got congress to approve the sale of war material to Britain on a lend lease program. They got rid of that bunch of old destroyers through lend lease. We were just months from Pearl Harbor and the congress was sitting on its hands. I think this is the time America was considered to be an isolationist nation. It was the time that I think America was at its lowest noble point in its history. And I do believe that a nation can be immoral or moral. I'm not the only one who can be as far behind the times as a dinosaur.

Our family had a kid in Idabel high school continuously for the next 12 years. For the last few years, we lived across the street from the high school. That was handy, John and Reynolds were coming along great and would be in high school very soon. They were active in all the social and sports events at school. John was playing basket and base ball. Both were playing in the band. Jerry was getting old enough to make his mark, his choice was football. In his junior and senior year he was doing an outstanding job as a linebacker. He was becoming the athlete of the family.

* * * * * *

I graduated from high school in 1940. The following school year, I enrolled in a southeastern state college in Tishimingo. I was majoring in science. I also worked as the helper to the band director. I was his "gofor". At least I was able to attend school. My parents gave me $2.00 a week to spend on foolishness and school supplies and personal upkeep, sometime

I got it and sometime I didn't. That was a pretty good allowance, considering there was very little foolishness going on in Tishimingo.

At Tishimingo we had a very strict code when it came to the boy, girl thing. The girls lined up every afternoon, about 6 o' clock, and walked down town, about a mile or so, and went to the picture show. The boys walked across the street from them and paralleled the trip to the picture show. Of course there were a lot of cat calls and hoorah's and loud talking exchanged from one side of the road to the other. Boys weren't allowed in the girls dormitory except for one hour in the evening, even then you had to sit in the lobby.

Tishimingo it'self may not really be located in Little Dixie, but most of the kids that went there were from our part of the state. I got the signal from that most of the kids were subjected to much the same discipline as we were in our home. As I look back, that kind of control really must have heightened the expectancy and reward of sneaking an experimental kiss in a darkened theater. There were a lot of attempts to circumvent the rules. But not too many of them were successful.

Just because we all were a little shy about hand holding, doesn't mean that the boys were retarded and backwards. We had a very strict and somewhat violent introduction into the world of higher education. We had a very active hazing period from the beginning of school until Thanksgiving. Our upper classmen were "el supreme-o's" during that time.

To start the first week off, the upperclassmen would form two lines facing each other that stretched the full length of the football field, from goal post to goal post.for this game. About the 3rd or 4th night we were there, all the freshmen were rousted out of the dormitories to run the full length of that line, while the upper classmen whacked you with their leather belts as you passed by them. Let me tell you, you gained speed for the full length. By the time you reached the other goal post you were going at least 50 miles an hour.

There was a way that you could minimize the pain and suffering. I thought of it after the 2nd step I took. I ran up really close to one side of the line. The boys on that side were too close to you to be really effective. The guys on the opposite side were too far away to hit you. It had one little weakness; the guys further down the line began to back away from your path so they could get a better swing at you. When I saw the line ahead of me backing off, I just switched over to the other side. And I was ok for a good long distance. When I came out between the far goal post, I bet I hadn't been hit more than 4 or 5 times with a good solid whack in that whole distance.

After the last freshman came through, the whole affair turned into a big gang fight. It was us against them. The only problem was that you didn't know the freshmen from the upper classmen, so you hit everybody. That was lots of fun.

I had no hard feelings about the whole hazing program. But we had to wear a damn little green cap at all times outside of our room. I think that tradition came from the colleges in our "movver" country, England. The girls thought we were crazy, the faculty was concerned it would get out of hand. I didn't understand why it was necessary, but as long as it was part of college, I was going to get all I could out of it. It got pretty rough at times, especially if you rebelled or challenged the upper classmen. Also, part of it was silly. For instance, 3 or 4 of us lower classmen had to stand and sing the old religious song named "further along", over and over, for two solid hours while our upper classmen studied their lessons for the next day. We sounded awful, but they didn't care and neither did we.

The only requirement that we had from the upper-classmen was, we had to put "feeling" in it.

When we broke for thanksgiving holiday, we all threw our green caps out into the yard in one violent act of contempt. They found one cap that some old boy had done his business in. I guess he had a bad experience being a freshman or at least he had a bad attitude about it.

One day one of the guys showed up in the dormitory with his ankle all taped up walking on a set of crutches. Of course everyone wanted to know what happened. But he would not say a word about that. Oh, he would say it wasn't anything! He just twisted it. Finally we all got the story through the grapevine. He had persuaded his girl friend to take a rope up to her room one night. She lived on the second floor of the dormitory. The plan was that she would let the rope down and he would climb up the rope later that night. So far so good. But, as you know, "the best laid plan", when he was almost all the way up to her room, she suddenly changed her mind and untied or cut the rope. Well, he fell to the ground and broke his ankle. That's what we heard . His final story was that he dropped a milk can on it. He never did admit to the rope thing.

Another weird episode happened. This one is true. Several of us witnessed part of it. One of the girls dormitory was designed like a big two story home. It had a roof over a big front porch. The top of the porch roof was about 5 or 6 feet below a row of windows in the girls rooms.

Early one morning they heard a girl crying out for help toward the front of the house. The dorm mother went outside and there was this girl upon the porch roof in utter distress. What had happened, they surmised, she was going to sneak out on the roof, then down to the ground and go on a date. Well, she dropped out of her window onto the roof, then she couldn't get down on the ground and the window was too high for her to climb back into her room. She had spent the whole night there. We never did find out the names of the persons involved, oh well, just “another” well laid plan that went wrong.

* * * * * *

World war 11 was underway in Europe. There was no way that we could stay out of it. I was still a little too young for the army but the draft could not be put off very long. I was getting close to the perfect age to be drafted into service. So a buddy of mine and I were debating as to whether or not it would be wise to go ahead and volunteer. Then we could have our choice of the branch of service we wanted. This was “big decision” time in our lives. It seemed a certainty that we would be leaving college and our homes, and Little Dixie very soon.

My little brothers were only a year or two from having to make the same decision for themselves. WW1 had lasted several years. So would this one last a long time. Once in a while I would wonder about what they would do when their time came to decide the same questions. We had always been taught that “not to go when called”, would bring dishonor on our family. That seemed to me to be self evident.

To me it was a question of which branch I would choose, the army air corps or the navy air corp. Having an uncle in the navy, flying the PBY patrol boat, was a strong pull in that direction.

John, the next oldest boy, was leaning toward the marine corps. He was the one with “steady nerves” in our family. When we lived in Valliant, Oklahoma, he was about 7 or 8 years old, the thing for us big boys (13 and 14 year olds) to do, was to climb upon the top of the big water tower at the edge of town. It was 150 to 200 feet tall. We would climb up the ladder that was built into one of the 4 legs of the tower. We would then get up on the walkway around the thing and smoke cigarettes, chew tobacco and spit off the top and try to hit a target on the ground. Some of the guys even did their business off the platform and tried to hit a little concrete slab at the base of the tower. It was a place to let your inhibitions run wild.

John wanted to be one of the big boys, so he smoked a camel cigarette before he started his adventure. He figured this stunt would require that he have "steady nerves". At that time camel cigaretts were advertising, if you smoked their brand you would have "steady nerves". So he had a few drags off one, then he climbed to the top of that tank, on the diagonal round rods that criss-crossed between the legs. He came all the way, hand over hand and leg over leg, to the underside of the walk around platform, then he made his way around the structure until he got up on top of the walkway. We didn't know how he had managed to get on the walkway until he showed us his route and announced he was able to do that because he had smoked a camel and now he had "steady nerves". We made him use the ladder coming down.

* * * * * *

My time in the Little Dixie country was coming to an end. The depression had given way to the prosperity generated by the clouds of war that hung over the country as well as the whole world. No one knew how our childhood experiences, during the depression, poverty and disadvantaged periods, would help or hurt our development as adults. We didn't know that we had been poor or had gone to schools that had little or nothing to teach except the 3 r's. There were no well equipped science laboratories, no electronic aids such as video, tv's or computers. We had little or no exposure to the arts , or music, other than the bands. We really were limited to the basics. However they were emphasized and driven in with a lot of fervor.

I guess each kid in the whole country developed along his own chosen path. Emily Jean, no. 2 in the family sequence, wanted every thing around the house to be pretty and be well organized, clean and in it's right place. Right there was her problem. With all those boys to contend with. They wanted everything scattered around so it would be handy in case you needed it. Whether it was pretty or not didn't matter, just so long as it hung together and would work it was ok. Ever so often, mother would have to thump a few guys heads to keep Jean from wiping up the floor with a boy or two. She was a big help for mother on the inside work. The girls did the inside work and the boys sometime took care of the outside.

Jean did not know if we had a cow or not, and she would not have recognized it if she had seen it downtown. She helped mother when they wanted to "redo" a piece of furniture or repaint a room. She was a really good pianist. She could play classical music and popular music. I would get her to play something classical once in a while and I would sit really quite and peaceful so I could enjoy a little culture and class.

When she graduated from high school, the exodus from the country side into Washington DC had begun. She and 4 or 5 other girls, in her class, decided to go to washington and work in government to help in the war effort. So they all packed up their things, got on a bus, and headed up north out of Little Dixie. They all got jobs immediately and stayed in washington until the war ended. I think that most of the original group had met the boy of their dreams and when they left washington they started getting married. Jean had met and eventually married a soldier named Earl Jolly from california. He had spent about 4 years in England in the eight air force. When they all were released from their government jobs, the shift to civilian careers began. Earl went to work for United airlines, Jean's career became her family, children and grandchildren and she is still happily and actively doing it.

The day that John was 18 years old he was standing at the front door of the courthouse, waiting for the marine recruiting office to open up. He was in the 4th marines and took part in 4 or 5 different island invasions that were among the major battles in the pacific. He survived two almost complete wipeouts of the members of his platoon. I guess he still had "steady nerves", and I know he still does to this day.

He was eventually wounded on Siapan. He was the only one in the family that got a purple heart. Then again, he was wounded on Iwo Jima and got another purple heart. Heck, he was the only one in the family that got two purple hearts. Afterwards,if we started telling about our war stories , all of us other guys clamed up and let John talk. We have no stories that can compete with his. Dad would tell us to all hush up and let John talk.

After discharge from the marines, John got a degree in agriculture from Oklahoma state university in Stillwater Oklahoma . He married edna caldwell from Valliant Oklahoma . She graduated from the university of Oklahoma with a math degree. She was his long time sweetheart. After graduation, she became a math teacher. John became a teacher for trainees on the GI bill for farming in Nebraska. After a few years as a teacher, he went to work for and finally retired from the Swift company in Kansas City, Kansas.

Reynolds, the 3rd. boy child, joined the navy the day he was of age, which happened to be about 2 or 3 weeks before he got his diploma from high school, but the principle told him to go ahead and join. His grade point average was so high , they would send him his diploma after school was out.

He was the professor of the family. He went to the electronic school in the navy and became the radio operator on one of the navy's big flying boats that patrolled for submarines in and around the Bermuda triangle area. I think it was the consolidated aircraft company PB2y, a huge 4 engine long range seaplane.

After his navy flying career, he married an Idabel girl, Catherine Charles. He taught electronics in service schools before discharge from the navy. He then attended Oklahoma university and received a degree in physics. He continued in the field and taught and wrote technical training books in electronics at Lowery airforce base in Denver Colorado for a while. He then completed his career as a director at Hughes aircraft co, in the missile and space computer and guidance division in Santa Monica California.

The little girl Mozelle, who was no. 5 child. Became the ramrod of all the kids her size that lived in Idabel. When the family's discipline mechanism broke down, she took over and ran it single handed. She whipped every kid in the neighborhood, boys and girls. She got her training by being raised in the midst of 5 boys. She had to learn to take care of herself, and home was a good training ground.

After we all were grown, one day we were having coffee at the cafe downtown. A great big old rough boy about 6'2" around 240lbs came up to the table and asked if she was Mozelle Gardner, she said, yes she was. He introduced himself and she recognized him and introduced him to the rest of the group. He then asked Mozelle "do you want to try and whip me now"? He laughed and told us the last time he had seen Mozelle, she was chasing him home as fast as he could run.

She and her husband Albert Alexandra, a Tennessee boy, have retired and she is active in the Eastern Star organization. Albert is very active in the Free Masons.

Later in our lives, Mozelle and Albert were the angels of mercy and the primary care givers to our mother when she could no longer live alone and or take care of herself. They made arrangements to provide her with a home next to theirs. They managed and supervised her full time, live- in nursing care and provide her personal and medical needs for a number of years. All of the family will be forever grateful and thankfull to them for that.

Jerry Drew, no.4 son, joined the airforce as soon as he became of age. He applied for and was accepted in the air force aviation cadet corps to be a pilot. He graduated and became an f-86 jet fighter pilot. He had also gone through the phases of wanting to be a pilot above all other careers, like I did. He was the proper one. He would not write nor even cash a counter check, or carry a load of brown paper bags with groceries in them. That was not dignified.

After he served his tour in the airforce, he enrolled at the university of Oklahoma for a degree in electrical engineering. He had married an Idabel girl, Felecia Stout, while he was still in service. He was a captain in the active air force reserves, flying the f-86 jet fighter as a "week end warrior". He was on a night intercept training mission, when suddenly he disappeared from radar. There was never a word or warning of any kind of impending danger. The next day, they found him near El Reno Oklahoma. He had crashed. They never did find the cause.

All the kids came home to attend the funeral. It was a sad and sorrowful day. All 5 of the boys had served during WW11. I flew Bombers in the Eighth air force in England. John was in the 4th marines in the pacific. After the war, mother told us she had worried God to death about her boys, and she promised him that, if he would help her get them all back home, she would never bother him again. Mother had lost her brother, the navy pilot at pearl harbor within a week or so after the war started . Dad had died in 1953 while I was on reserve active duty during the korean war.

With Dad's and Jerry's deaths— that was the beginning, we were paying the bitter, bitter price that father time eventually extracts from all of us. During the burial service for Jerry, while we were in the private "family room" at the funeral home, every one of us were so quite in our grief that you could hear your heart beat. I could feel mother sitting next to me, silently sobbing and shaking inside. I knew she was having a hard time keeping her composure. She turned toward to me and said. "I wanted to hold him in my arms— just one more time— before I gave him up".

This was the first time that a major disaster had struck our immediate family. Up until that time, we had one appendicitis operation for Emily Jean, when she was about 6 years old. John Pascal had broken a collar bone. He was run over by a tricycle when he was about 3 years old. One arm broken for Reynolds. He fell out of a wagon loaded with peaches when he was 2 or 3 years old. Our family has been fortunate. I'm sure we have spent no more than 5 hundred dollars on all the family docter and medical bills up until we were all grown.

The youngest and no. 5 son, Walter Cleveland, joined the Airforce when he got out of high school and served his tour in Germany. He was too young for the war, but he got to go overseas during the occupation of Germany. He specialized in radio communications. At that time the americans were monitoring and recording the secret military communications being transmitted by the communist from deep in Russia. He was one of the guys who actually copied down the coded messages by hand, then they were sent to our national intelligence agencies.

After he was discharged, he enrolled in Oklahoma State university in Stillwater and received his degree in geology. When he graduated, he and his wife, a German girl named Rosey Kuhn went to live in California. They are now retired and moved backed to Little Dixie.

I got my degree in aeronautical engineering at Oklahoma university in 1948. I spent most of my career at Cape Canaveral in the missile and space programs for Mc Donnell Douglas aircraft co. I married Nancy Herd, from Swink, Oklahoma in 1946. I retired from Douglas aircraft in 1977 and now live near the heart of Little Dixie, the town of Mena, Arkansas.

That is pretty much the pattern for all our family. All of us have had great, fullfilling careers scattered all over the country. Now most of us have moved back to Little Dixie, from whence we came, with the exception of Emily Jean. Her husband is the native Californian. They have settled down in California, where all their kids live.

None of the seven kids ever got a divorce. None were ever arrested or sent to the little solid concrete iron reinforced jail. In spite of all the supposed ill effects of poverty and the lack of the advantages of life here in Little Dixie. I think we will now agree that we allways have been living very close to the reality of the Simpson's kids vision of the Indian's "happy hunting ground"

End

H. Tom Gardner

About the Author

The oldest son in a family of 7, who, despite the hardships of growing up a new state, Oklahoma, an area hit hard by the Depression, went on to obtain a college degree, become a combat pilot in WWII and spent the next 20 years with the space program at Cape Kennedy, Florida

www.ingramcontent.com/pod-product-compliance
Ingram Content Group UK Ltd.
Pitfield, Milton Keynes, MK11 3LW, UK
UKHW040559210726
13854UKWH00008B/1551

9 780759 626270